Children's Illustrat
Animal
ATLAS

Author Jamie Ambrose

Editor Olivia Stanford

Project editor Allison Singer

Project art editor Hoa Luc

Designer Rhea Gaughan

Map illustrator Jeongeun Park

Cartography Ed Merritt, Simon Mumford

Illustrators Maltings Partnership, Molly Lattin, Bettina Myklebust Stovne, Oliver Magee

Additional design Lucy Sims, Yamini Panwar

Assistant editor Prerna Grewal

Jacket co-ordinator Francesca Young

Jacket designer Hoa Luc

Managing editor Laura Gilbert

Managing art editor Diane Peyton Jones

Pre-production producer Nikoleta Parasaki

Producer Niamh Tierney

Art director Martin Wilson

Publisher Sarah Larter

Publishing director Sophie Mitchell

First published in Great Britain in 2017 by
Dorling Kindersley Limited
80 Strand, London, WC2R 0RL

A CIP catalogue record for this book
is available from the British Library

ISBN: 978-0-2412-8385-1

Printed and bound in Hong Kong

A WORLD OF IDEAS:
SEE ALL THERE IS TO KNOW

Contents

4 How to use this book

6 The world

8 North America

10 North American taiga

12 Great Plains

13 Eastern forests

14 Western deserts

16 Central America

17 Caribbean

18 Florida Everglades

20 South America

22 Amazon rainforest

24 Andean mountains

26 Temperate pampas

28 Pantanal

29 Galápagos

30 Cerrado

32 Cordillera Blanca

34 Africa

36 Sahara Desert

38 Congo Basin

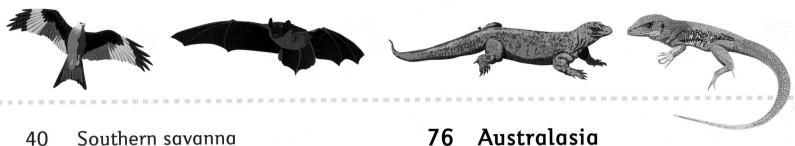

40 Southern savanna

42 Kalahari Desert

43 Madagascar

44 Kruger National Park

46 Europe

48 Northern European taiga

50 British Isles

52 European forests

54 The Alps

55 European steppe

56 Mediterranean scrubland

58 Białowieża Forest

60 Asia

62 Russian taiga

64 Asian steppe

65 Central Asian deserts

66 Tibetan Plateau

68 East Asian forests

70 Arabian Peninsula

71 Indian forests

72 Southeast Asian rainforest

74 Gobi Desert

76 Australasia

78 Australia

80 New Zealand

82 Great Barrier Reef

84 Antarctica

86 The Arctic

88 Oceans and seas

90 Atlas picture quiz

92 Glossary

93 Index

96 Credits

How to use this book

An atlas usually shows maps of different countries, but animals often live across borders. The maps in this book show many of the world's different habitats, which is the environment where an animal lives, such as a desert. Some islands are also shown, as they have animals that are found nowhere else.

Compass
The compass always points north (N) in line with the map. It also shows the direction of south (S), east (E), and west (W).

Animal pictures
Pictures with descriptions pick out particular animals that live in an area.

Independent states
Small independent states, such as Monaco, are shown with a red border and a solid red dot, and the name is in capital letters.

Rivers
Each country's largest rivers are shown as continuous blue lines.

Mediterranean scrubland

The coastal areas around the Mediterranean Sea contain rocky hills and flat, shrub-filled plains. This rare habitat is found in only a few places on Earth. Plants here can survive wildfires, and animals have to cope with hot, dry weather.

Mediterranean chameleon
This is one of only two chameleon species found in Europe. Its tongue is sticky to catch passing insects, and is so long that it is twice the length of its body!

Hummingbird hawk moth
This insect beats its wings so fast that they make a humming sound — just like the birds it's named after. It feeds on nectar made by flowers like buddleia and honeysuckle.

The hawk moth will return to a nectar-rich flower day after day.

Iberian lynx
Just 404 adult Iberian lynxes are left in the wild, so this is the most endangered cat on Earth — but the good news is this figure is nearly twice the number of wild lynxes alive a few years ago!

This cat mainly hunts just one animal – the European rabbit.

This wolf is thinner and smaller than other European wolves. It hunts rabbits, deer, wild boar, birds, and fish.

FRANCE

CROATIA — Zagreb

MONACO

SAN MARINO

The golden jackal is found in lots of places, including southeastern Europe, northern Africa, and southern Asia.

Golden jackal

Belgrade

ROMANIA

BOSNIA & HERZEGOVINA — Sarajevo

SERBIA

ITALY

Garonne

Rhône

PYRENEES

ANDORRA

Iberian wolf

SPAIN

Ebro

Mediterranean banded centipede
This centipede paralyzes its prey with a venomous bite and will give a human a painful nip too – so stay well away!

Mediterranean tree frog
This frog is usually bright green or blue. It has suckers on its fingers and toes that let it climb with ease.

Corsica

Sardinia

VATICAN CITY

Rome

The cork oak is one of few trees that can grow new bark. The cork bark is harvested once every nine years to make bottle stoppers and other items.

Cork oak

MONTENEGRO — Podgorica

Pristina

KOSOVO — Skopje

Tirana

MACEDONIA

ALBANIA

BULGARIA

ADRIATIC SEA

PORTUGAL

Madrid

Tagus

Jewelled lizard

Majorca

The cuckoo lays its eggs in other birds' nests. When the cuckoo chick hatches, it pushes all the other eggs out – so the parent birds feed it instead!

Common cuckoo

The magpie is so clever that it can make and use tools. It eats insects and seeds, and will even steal other birds' eggs.

Magpie

As well as making other sounds, this pelican barks and hisses! When fishing, it fills up its beak with food to eat later.

Dalmatian pelican

GREECE

Marginated tortoise

Athens

Lisbon

This monkey is found in Africa and on the island of Gibraltar, near Spain. It is the only wild monkey in Europe.

The sapphire-like blue spots on its body give this lizard its name. It is the largest lizard in Europe at about 60 cm (23½ in) long.

Iberian ibex

Iberian pig

This pig is a farmed animal, but lives in open country, looking for mushrooms, roots, and acorns from cork oaks.

Barbary macaque

A type of wild goat, male Iberian ibexes have horns that grow up to 75 cm (29½ in) long!

MEDITERRANEAN SEA

Sicily

This plant-eating tortoise lives mainly in Greece, in thorny, rocky, scrubby areas.

MEDITERRANEAN SEA

Crete

HABITAT KEY
- Scrublands
- Wetlands
- Mountains
- Coniferous forests
- Deciduous forests

SCALE

| 0 | 200 miles |
| 0 | 200 kilometres |

European rabbit
The European rabbit is the ancestor of all pet rabbits in the world. Unlike its enemy, the Iberian lynx, the rabbit has been seen in gardens and parks, and even in busy cities.

Location
This region includes the southern parts of Europe around the Mediterranean Sea, as well as islands like Crete that share a similar habitat.

Mediterranean house gecko
This little gecko is about 10 cm (4 in) long and weighs about as much as a sugar cube. It is also called a "moon lizard" because it mainly comes out at night. It eats small cockroaches and moths.

Capital
A country's capital city is marked with a red outline. Some countries have more than one capital city.

Scale
The scale shows the size of the areas and the distances between different points on the map.

Location
The location box shows you where each area is found in relation to the land around it.

Habitat key
Every map has a key that lists the types of habitats found in that area.

Bordering continents
Around the edges of some maps you can see parts of bordering continents in a cream colour.

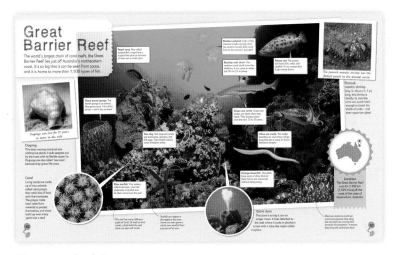

Continent maps

The continent maps are coloured to show the biomes found on each continent. A biome is a large area of one type of habitat, and the animals and plants in it. Photographs show some of the places in these biomes.

Feature habitats

The feature spreads show a specific place and some of the animals that live there. In reality, not all the animals would be found together at the same time, as they are awake at different times of day, and would often avoid each other to prevent being eaten!

Habitats

These symbols show the different types of habitat on each map.

Hot desert
Hot deserts, such as the Sahara, are dry, sandy areas and few plants grow here.

Cold desert
Cold deserts, such as the Gobi, are cold, dry stretches of land.

Snow and ice
Frozen areas are found high up in the mountains and at the North and South Poles.

Mountains
High, rugged mountainous areas are often covered with snow.

Oceans and seas
Huge stretches of water are found around the Earth's seven continents.

Tropical forests
Rainforests, such as the Amazon, get a lot of rain and heat so the trees grow very tall.

Deciduous forests
Trees in deciduous forests usually have broad leaves that are lost in autumn, or during the dry season.

Coniferous forests
Trees in coniferous forests usually have needle-like leaves that are kept all year round.

Mangroves
Mangrove trees grow on coasts in salty water. Their long roots stick out of the water.

Coral reefs
Coral reefs grow in shallow waters. They are built by coral animals.

Scrublands
Low-lying plants and grasses grow in scrubland areas with small trees, such as in southern Spain.

Wetlands
Wetlands are marshy, swampy areas, such as the Pantanal in Brazil.

Temperate grasslands
Flat, grassy plains with few trees found in seasonal areas are temperate grasslands, such as prairie, steppe, and pampas.

Tropical grasslands
Flat, grassy plains with few trees found in hot areas are tropical grasslands, such as savanna and cerrado.

Borders

Borders show how the Earth's land is divided into countries.

Country borders
The borders between countries are shown with a white broken line.

Disputed borders
Some countries disagree about where the border between them should be. These borders are shown with a white dotted line.

Continent borders
A broken orange line shows where the border is between two continents.

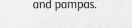

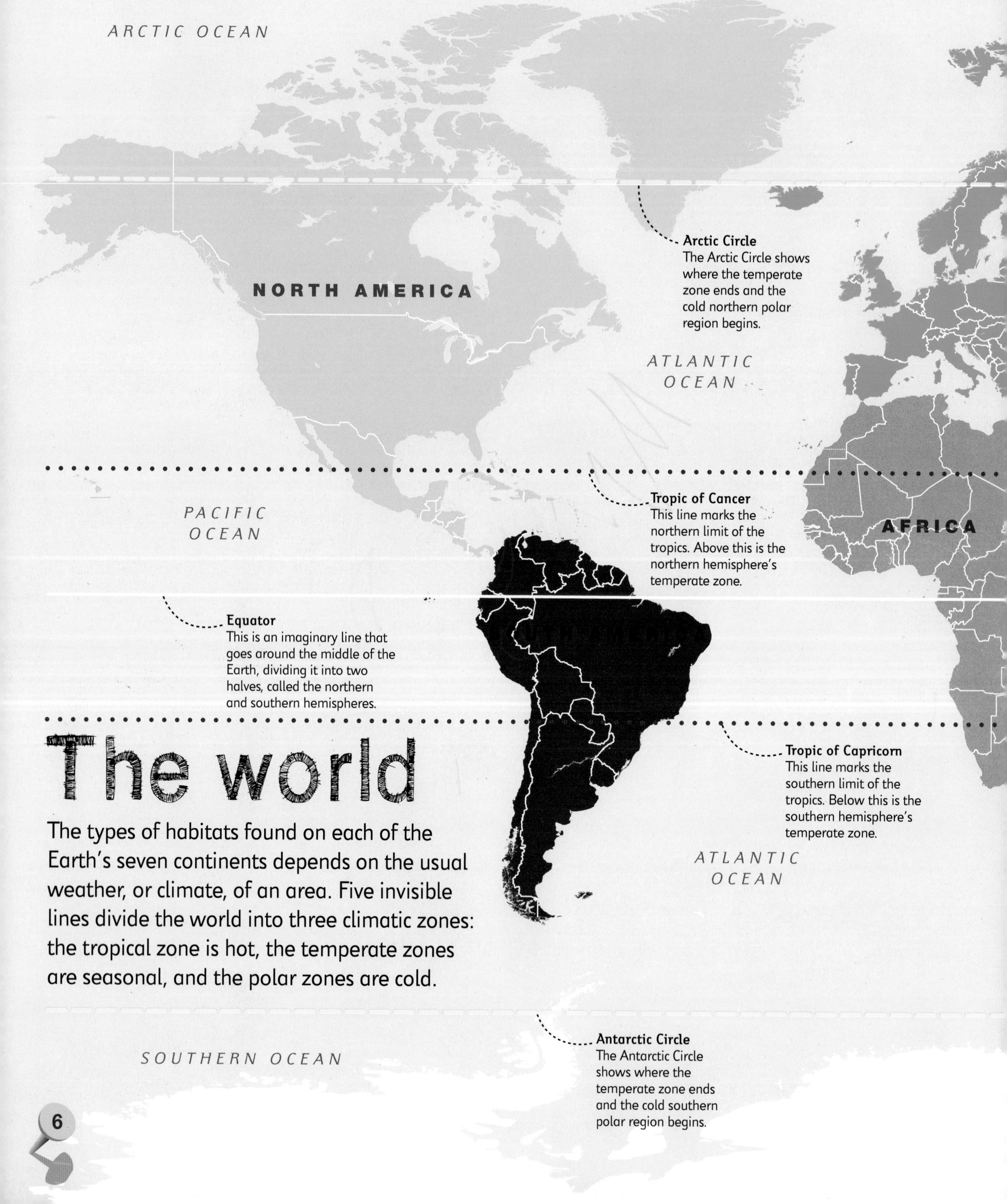

ARCTIC OCEAN

NORTH AMERICA

ATLANTIC OCEAN

Arctic Circle
The Arctic Circle shows where the temperate zone ends and the cold northern polar region begins.

PACIFIC OCEAN

Tropic of Cancer
This line marks the northern limit of the tropics. Above this is the northern hemisphere's temperate zone.

AFRICA

Equator
This is an imaginary line that goes around the middle of the Earth, dividing it into two halves, called the northern and southern hemispheres.

The world

The types of habitats found on each of the Earth's seven continents depends on the usual weather, or climate, of an area. Five invisible lines divide the world into three climatic zones: the tropical zone is hot, the temperate zones are seasonal, and the polar zones are cold.

Tropic of Capricorn
This line marks the southern limit of the tropics. Below this is the southern hemisphere's temperate zone.

ATLANTIC OCEAN

Antarctic Circle
The Antarctic Circle shows where the temperate zone ends and the cold southern polar region begins.

SOUTHERN OCEAN

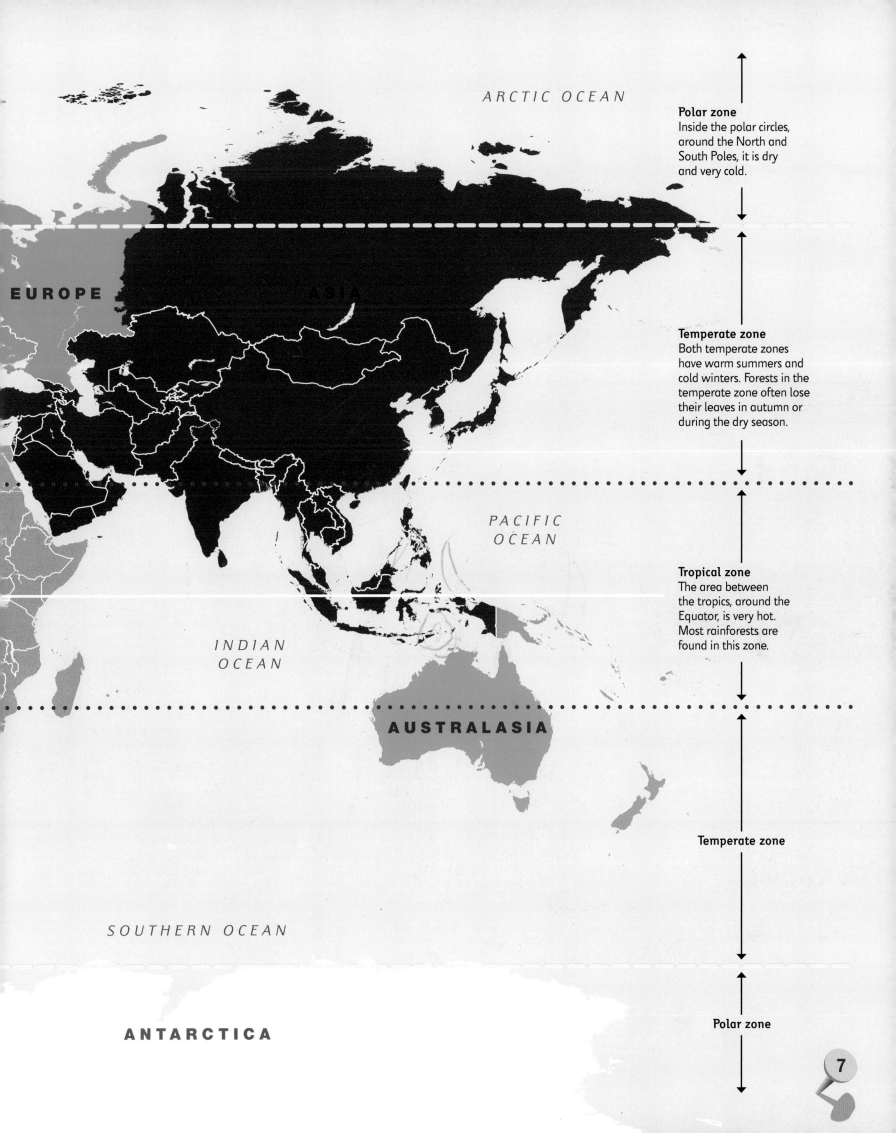

ARCTIC OCEAN

EUROPE

ASIA

PACIFIC
OCEAN

INDIAN
OCEAN

AUSTRALASIA

SOUTHERN OCEAN

ANTARCTICA

Polar zone
Inside the polar circles, around the North and South Poles, it is dry and very cold.

Temperate zone
Both temperate zones have warm summers and cold winters. Forests in the temperate zone often lose their leaves in autumn or during the dry season.

Tropical zone
The area between the tropics, around the Equator, is very hot. Most rainforests are found in this zone.

Temperate zone

Polar zone

North America

This continent stretches from the icy Arctic down to the tropical Caribbean. It has a vast range of habitats, from snow-covered mountains to lush rainforests, and is home to millions of different animals — some large, some small, and all amazing.

ARCTIC OCEAN

BEAUFORT SEA

BERING SEA

ALASKA
(UNITED STATES)

Yukon Territory

Northwest Territories

PACIFIC OCEAN

British Columbia

Alberta

Washington

Montana

Oregon

Idaho

UNITED STATE

Nevada

Utah

California

Arizona

Western mountains

The rocky peaks and thick coniferous forests in the mountains of western North America are filled with wildlife. Wolves, deer, and grizzly bears roam freely here, while in the fjords (narrow inlets), bald eagles hunt for salmon.

HAWAII
(UNITED STATES)

California coast redwoods

These redwood trees can grow more than 107 m (350 ft) high and live up to 2,000 years. Bears, owls, and other woodland creatures — including a banana slug — call them home.

Great Plains

With thousands of kilometres of grassland, the dry Great Plains can appear empty. Look closer, though, and you'll see big bison, as well as prairie dogs hiding in their secret world of underground burrows.

HABITAT KEY

- Tropical forests
- Deciduous forests
- Coniferous forests
- Tropical grasslands
- Scrublands
- Temperate grasslands
- Desert
- Wetlands
- Tundra
- Ice
- Mangroves

GREENLAND
(DENMARK)

CANADA

Nunavut

Newfoundland & Labrador

Manitoba

Québec

Saskatchewan

Ontario

Prince Edward Island

New Brunswick

Nova Scotia

ST PIERRE & MIQUELON
(FRANCE)

Maine

North Dakota

Minnesota

Wisconsin

Vermont

New Hampshire

New York

Massachusetts

South Dakota

Michigan

Rhode Island

Connecticut

Nebraska

Iowa

Illinois

Indiana

Ohio

Pennsylvania

New Jersey

Delaware

Maryland

OF AMERICA (USA)

West Virginia

Virginia

orado

Kansas

Missouri

Kentucky

North Carolina

BERMUDA
(UNITED KINGDOM)

New Mexico

Oklahoma

Arkansas

Tennessee

South Carolina

Mississippi

Alabama

Georgia

Texas

Louisiana

Florida

ATLANTIC OCEAN

GULF OF MEXICO

BAHAMAS

BRITISH VIRGIN ISLANDS
(UNITED KINGDOM)

ANGUILLA (UNITED KINGDOM)

ST KITTS & NEVIS

MEXICO

CUBA

PUERTO RICO
(UNITED STATES)

ANTIGUA & BARBUDA

MONTSERRAT (UNITED KINGDOM)

HAITI

DOMINICAN REPUBLIC

US VIRGIN ISLANDS
(UNITED STATES)

DOMINICA

MARTINIQUE (FRANCE)

BARBADOS

JAMAICA

ST LUCIA

GRENADA

ST VINCENT & THE GRENADINES

CARIBBEAN SEA

CURACAO
(NETHERLANDS)

TRINIDAD & TOBAGO

BELIZE

ARUBA
(NETHERLANDS)

GUATEMALA

HONDURAS

EL SALVADOR

NICARAGUA

COSTA RICA

PANAMA

Barrier islands

These long, thin stretches of sand protect the mainland from powerful storms. The barrier islands off the Virginia and Maryland coasts are home to the wild Chincoteague Ponies of Chincoteague and Assateague islands.

Central American rainforest

Rainforests are warm and green all year, and they are home to more than half the world's plants and animals. These colourful scarlet macaws from Costa Rica perch high in rainforest trees.

SCALE

0   500 miles   1000 miles

0   1000 kilometres

9

HABITAT KEY

Temperate grasslands

Coniferous forests

Mountains

Deciduous forests

ARCTIC OCEAN

BEAUFORT SEA

These large brown bears use their powerful jaws to snap up salmon in rivers and streams.

Alaska (USA)

Yukon

Mackenzie

Arctic Circle

Grizzly bear

Great Bear Lake

Pelly

Related to raspberries, this wild berry is eaten by many animals, including birds, bears – and people!

Great Slave Lake

Sea otters are found in shallow waters. Their thick fur keeps them warm in the sea.

ROCKY MOUNTAINS

Sea otter

Salmonberry

Leatherback turtle

COAST MOUNTAINS

The largest sea turtle in the world swims long distances across the Pacific, Indian, and Atlantic oceans.

Sockeye salmon

PACIFIC OCEAN

Salmon in the sea return to the freshwater streams they hatched in when it is time to lay their own eggs.

American badger

With big front feet and long claws, this animal digs burrows up to 10 m (32 ft) long.

North American taiga

Taiga areas are made of coniferous, or evergreen, forests that grow in some of the northernmost parts of the world. Grizzly bears and grey wolves live in the vast taiga of North America, which stretches across Canada, the world's second-largest country, and Alaska, the USA's largest state.

Location

Most of northern North America is taiga. Summer temperatures reach only 10°C (50°F), and there's lots of snow in the winter.

Great grey owl
North America's tallest owl has a wingspan of up to 1.5 m (5 ft). It listens for rodents moving under the snow, then snatches them up.

Snow geese
Flocks of snow geese turn fields white when they land. These noisy birds live in cold areas, but fly south in large groups during the winter.

Snow geese fly south for the winter.

HUDSON BAY

This flat-tailed mammal fells trees with its teeth. It uses the logs to build dams across rivers, and lodges to live in.

The loon's legs are made for swimming, not walking — so when it wants to fly, it can only take off from water.

A moose can weigh as much as a car! It can also trot at a steady pace of 32 kph (20 mph).

Pacific loon

American beaver

These geese are found all over the world. They have a loud honk and fly in a V-shaped formation.

CANADA

Moose

Both male and female fireflies flash yellow, green, or orange light using special organs in their tails.

Lake Winnipeg

Canada goose

Each winter, millions of monarchs migrate from northern North America to Mexico.

Monarch butterfly

Ottowa

Lake Superior

Firefly

Lake Huron

Lake Ontario

USA

Lake Michigan

Lake Erie

GULF OF ST LAWERENCE

ATLANTIC OCEAN

Grey wolf
The grey wolf is the largest wild member of the dog family. It can have black, white, tan, brown, or grey fur. It hunts in packs and eats animals from tiny mice to huge moose.

Prairie rattlesnake

Though it is venomous, the prairie rattlesnake would rather flee than fight. It rattles its tail rings, making a sound that warns, "Stay away"!

The national symbol of the United States, this powerful bird mainly eats fish and water birds.

Bald eagle

Often called "buffalo", these shaggy plant-eaters are North America's biggest mammal and heaviest animal.

American bison

Location

The Great Plains stretch from the Rocky Mountains east to the Mississippi River, and from southern Canada to as far south as Texas.

This large hare changes from brown to white in winter, but its tail stays white all year.

Male prairie chickens inflate their orange neck sacs and raise their feathers to attract females.

Greater prairie chicken

White-tailed jack rabbit

Lake Superior

This shrub's flower spikes provide food for mammals and nectar for insects.

This cat-sized orange fox lives up to its name. It is a swift night-time hunter that can run 48 kph (30 mph).

Swift fox

Missouri

Mississippi

Prairie shoestring

Colorado

A coyote howls to alert others.

This deer-like antelope can see predators from 6 km (almost 4 miles) away, and can run for amazing distances.

Arkansas

Coyote

With excellent eyesight and hearing, and a good sense of smell, coyotes make great hunters. They howl to claim their territory and to tell other coyotes where they are.

SCALE

0   250 miles

0   250 kilometres

Pronghorn

N W E S

HABITAT KEY

Temperate grasslands

Coniferous forests

Deciduous forests

Mountains

Cold desert

Hot desert

Great Plains

The Great Plains are in the centre of North America. Made of high prairie about 4,800 km (3,000 miles) long, they were once home to thousands of bison and antelope. Today farmland has taken over much of the area, and mostly cattle herds wander the plains — but wildlife has found ways to survive.

Black-tailed prairie dog

These grass-eating rodents live in underground "prairie dog towns". They greet family with a kiss, and have different warning calls for different predators.

Grey fox

As big as a medium-sized dog, grey foxes live in broadleaf forests. They make their dens in hollow trees, and both parents care for the cubs.

Eastern forests

Deciduous and coniferous forests cover eastern North America. There are mountains and river valleys here, too. Animals have to be clever to survive in areas densely populated with humans.

If threatened, the skunk sprays a horrible-smelling musk from glands under its tail.

Sugar maples provide sap for maple syrup. Their leaves turn orange-gold and red in autumn.

Lake Superior

Raccoons are highly intelligent. They can live in towns or the country and will eat almost anything!

Lake Michigan

Only male deer grow antlers. White-tails often escape predators by swimming across lakes or rivers.

Striped skunk

SCALE

0 ——————— 250 miles

0 ——————— 250 kilometres

This bright-red bird can sing more than 24 songs. When courting, males offer females the best seeds.

Sugar maple

Ohio

Northern cardinal

Northern raccoon

White-tailed deer

Mississippi

Washington, D.C.

This is North America's only marsupial. It can outsmart danger by playing dead for up to four hours.

Great horned owl

Virginia opossum

ATLANTIC OCEAN

This large owl's feathery "horns" look like ears, but its real ears are much further down on its skull.

Despite their name, grey squirrels can also have white or reddish fur.

HABITAT KEY

Temperate grasslands	Coniferous forests
Tropical grasslands	Deciduous forests
Mountains	

N
W E
S

Grey squirrel

Double-jointed ankles help grey squirrels to scamper up and down trees. Their teeth never stop growing, so they have to wear them down on nuts and tree bark.

American black bear

Good swimmers and climbers, black bears feast on fruit, nuts, and roots, and sometimes ants and grubs. There are twice as many of them in the world as there are all other bear species combined.

Location

Most of the continent's eastern forests stretch from the Mississippi River Valley eastwards, all the way to the Atlantic Ocean.

13

Western deserts

Western North America has four deserts. These dry, sandy areas are hot during the day, but at night they can get very cold. Animals here must survive these tough conditions – and with very little water.

USA

A tortoise snacks on a desert plant.

Mohave desert tortoise
This desert tortoise can live for up to 50 years. It digs a burrow to avoid the desert heat, and it spends 95 per cent of its time there during the summer.

A short, or "bobbed", tail gives this wild cat its name. More than a million bobcats live in North America.

ROCKY MOUNTAINS

Bobcat

Desert broom
The desert broom's flowers provide sweet nectar for butterflies.

Colorado

A turkey vulture perches on a cactus.

Turkey vulture
Turkey vultures can't kill their own prey, so they eat animals that have already died instead. Animals that behave in this way are called scavengers.

Great Salt Lake

This lizard lives mainly underground. It has a venomous bite and eats eggs.

Gila monster

Snake

Bighorn sheep

The jackrabbit can run up to 48 kph (30 mph) and jump 6 m (20 ft) into the air.

Black-tailed jackrabbit

Male bighorns fight by crashing their big heads and horns together.

This big, hairy spider lines its desert burrow with silk to keep it from caving in.

Desert blonde tarantula

SIERRA NEVADA

Western diamondback rattlesnake

Each time a diamondback sheds its skin, it gets a new section added to its rattle.

Greater roadrunner

Roadrunners run up to 29 kph (18 mph) and are one of the few animals that eat rattlesnakes.

MEXICO

SIERRA MADRE ORIENTAL

Merriam's kangaroo rat

This big-footed rodent doesn't need to drink water. It gets moisture from the seeds it eats instead.

Ringtail

A relative of the raccoon, the ringtail can climb straight up cliffs, trees, and even prickly cacti!

Nine-banded armadillo

The only armadillo living in North America, this animal has a great sense of smell.

Mexico City

Location

The Great Basin Desert is the furthest north of the western deserts. It's followed by the Mojave, the Sonoran, and finally the Chihuahuan deserts.

SIERRA MADRE OCCIDENTAL

Saguaro cactus

Sharp spines cover this tree-sized cactus to prevent animals from eating it.

Elf owl

Just 15 cm (6 in) tall, North America's smallest owl plays dead if captured.

Costa's hummingbird

Found in the Mojave and Sonoran deserts, this tiny bird slows down its heart rate to survive cold nights.

N E S W

PACIFIC OCEAN

HABITAT KEY

- Temperate grasslands
- Coniferous forests
- Tropical grasslands
- Deciduous forests
- Scrublands
- Tropical forests
- Mountains
- Hot desert
- Cold desert

SCALE

0   250 miles

0   250 kilometres

Puma

Also called the cougar or mountain lion, this big cat hunts at night. It is a fast runner, a good swimmer, and an excellent jumper and climber.

15

Resplendent quetzal

BELIZE

Mexican kite swallowtail butterfly

These butterflies are named for their long wingtips that look like swallows' tails.

This monkey swings through the rainforest and can hang from branches by its tail.

This tiny bird's long, curved bill lets it sip nectar from inside rainforest flowers.

GUATEMALA

Guatemala City

HONDURAS

HABITAT KEY

Mangroves   Tropical forests

Mountains

Coniferous forests   Deciduous forests

Geoffroy's spider monkey

EL SALVADOR

A male quetzal's twin tail feathers are more than twice as long as its body.

Tegucigalpa

San Salvador

Bronzy hermit hummingbird

NICARAGUA

SCALE

0   100 miles

0   100 kilometres

PACIFIC OCEAN

Managua

Tayra

The tayra hunts small monkeys, rodents, and birds, but it also eats fruit and honey.

CARIBBEAN SEA

COSTA RICA

Sticky finger pads help this little frog cling to twigs and branches.

N
W   E
S

San José

Red-eyed tree frog

It may look more like a pig, but the tapir is related to horses.

PANAMA

Hoffmann's two-toed sloth
Two long claws on its front legs let this slow-moving sloth get around the rainforest. It spends almost its entire life upside down!

Baird's tapir   Panama City

Central America

Seven countries make up the narrow strip of land that is Central America. More than 1,500 different species of birds live here, and many more animals find food and shelter in its warm rainforests.

Ocelot
This fast cat's super sight and hearing help it to hunt rabbits and other small animals at night. During the day it rests in the trees, where its markings blend in among the leaves.

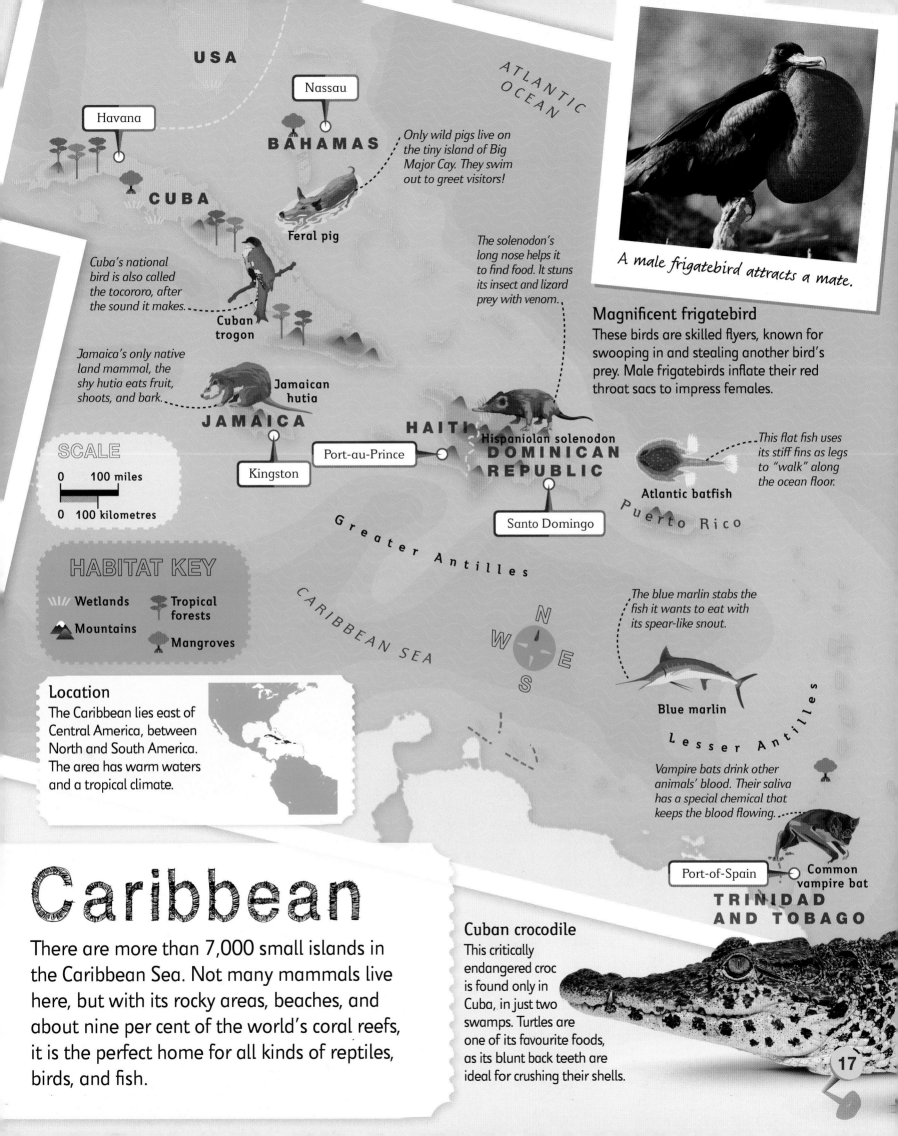

USA

Havana

Nassau

BAHAMAS

Only wild pigs live on the tiny island of Big Major Cay. They swim out to greet visitors!

CUBA

Feral pig

ATLANTIC OCEAN

The solenodon's long nose helps it to find food. It stuns its insect and lizard prey with venom.

A male frigatebird attracts a mate.

Cuba's national bird is also called the tocororo, after the sound it makes.

Cuban trogon

Magnificent frigatebird
These birds are skilled flyers, known for swooping in and stealing another bird's prey. Male frigatebirds inflate their red throat sacs to impress females.

Jamaica's only native land mammal, the shy hutia eats fruit, shoots, and bark.

Jamaican hutia

JAMAICA

HAITI

Hispaniolan solenodon

DOMINICAN REPUBLIC

Port-au-Prince

Kingston

This flat fish uses its stiff fins as legs to "walk" along the ocean floor.

Atlantic batfish

Puerto Rico

SCALE

0   100 miles

0   100 kilometres

Santo Domingo

Greater Antilles

CARIBBEAN SEA

HABITAT KEY

\\\|/ Wetlands

Tropical forests

Mountains

Mangroves

The blue marlin stabs the fish it wants to eat with its spear-like snout.

N
W   E
S

Blue marlin

Lesser Antilles

Location
The Caribbean lies east of Central America, between North and South America. The area has warm waters and a tropical climate.

Vampire bats drink other animals' blood. Their saliva has a special chemical that keeps the blood flowing.

Port-of-Spain

Common vampire bat

TRINIDAD AND TOBAGO

Caribbean

There are more than 7,000 small islands in the Caribbean Sea. Not many mammals live here, but with its rocky areas, beaches, and about nine per cent of the world's coral reefs, it is the perfect home for all kinds of reptiles, birds, and fish.

Cuban crocodile
This critically endangered croc is found only in Cuba, in just two swamps. Turtles are one of its favourite foods, as its blunt back teeth are ideal for crushing their shells.

Florida Everglades

The Everglades, North America's largest subtropical wetland, is really a big, slow-moving river. The area is half its original size due to humans sending its water to farms and cities. However, it is still home to 350 bird species, and reptiles such as alligators and crocodiles.

Common snapping turtle

Although it has no teeth, this turtle's strong, bony beak and jaws can bite and kill birds, fish, and small mammals. It is also known to bite the heads off other turtles that come too close. No wonder most animals, including humans, know to leave it alone!

Around 300 fish species are found in the waters of the Everglades, ranging from tiny pygmy sunfish to barracudas that can grow up to 2 m (6 ft) long.

Great blue heron North America's largest heron is a slow-mover, but it strikes fast to catch fish in mid-swim.

Anhinga This bird hunts underwater. It acts like a spearfisherman, stabbing fish with its long, sharp bill.

American alligator The Everglades is the only place in the wild where alligators and crocodiles live together.

A rat snake shows off its forked tongue.

Everglades rat snake

This long snake both swims and can climb trees. Rats are on its menu, but it also eats frogs, squirrels, and birds and their eggs.

An alligator's teeth are hidden from sight when its mouth is closed – unlike a crocodile's, which are always visible.

Everglades snail kite This bird of prey eats apple snails. It uses its curved bill to pull the snails out of their shells.

An orbweaver sits in wait on its web.

Golden silk orbweaver
Female orbweavers can grow up to 8 cm (3 in) long. Their silk is gold in colour, and it is stronger than the material used in bulletproof vests!

Purple gallinule This duck-sized bird has long toes that allow it to walk on lily pads without sinking.

Florida panther These panthers are critically endangered. Fewer than 100 are left in the wild, as so many have been hunted.

Location
The Everglades stretches across the southern tip of Florida. During its rainy season, this area gets twice as much rain as other places in the US.

Green tree frog
Depending on its mood, this little frog is either bright green or dull khaki in colour. It inflates its vocal sac and screams if picked up – which can save its life, as the scream makes a lot of predators drop it in surprise!

South America

Earth's fourth-largest continent lies mostly in the southern half of the world. It has tropical rainforests, dry deserts, grassy plains, and high, snowy mountains. The many different habitats means that a variety of amazing animals can make South America their home.

GALÁPAGOS
ISLANDS
(ECUADOR)

VENEZUELA

COLOMBIA

ECUADOR

PERU

BOLIVIA

Amazon rainforest
The winding Amazon River flows through the massive rainforest that shares its name. As well as producing a fifth of the planet's oxygen, this rainforest is home to an astonishing amount of plants, mammals, birds, and fish.

PACIFIC OCEAN

Pantanal
The Pantanal is a wetland wonderland. With flooded grasslands and tropical forests, it is home to thousands of birds, fish, and reptiles. Mammals also live here, such as the plant-eating capybara, which hides from predators in the muddy waters.

HABITAT KEY

- Tropical forests
- Deciduous forests
- Tropical grasslands
- Scrublands
- Temperate grasslands
- Deserts
- Wetlands
- Mountains
- Mangroves

CHILE

ARGENTINA

GUYANA

SURINAME

FRENCH
GUIANA
(FRANCE)

ATLANTIC OCEAN

BRAZIL

ARAGUAY

URUGUAY

FALKLAND ISLANDS
(UNITED KINGDOM)

Patagonian steppe

Shared between Argentina and southern
Chile, the warm, dry Patagonian steppe
is filled with shrubs as well as grasses.
It makes a good home for mammals,
ranging from tiny rodents to foxes
and mountain lions.

Pampas

Its acres of grassland mean
the pampas attracts a lot of
wildlife, particularly birds.
Some, like the flightless
Darwin's rhea, graze on
plants. It also eats frogs
and insects that might
be hiding in the grass.

Andes

Although parts are warm
with plenty of plants, the
Andean mountains are
mostly full of high, rugged
places. Animals need to be
tough and adaptable to live
here. Flamingos, for instance,
can manage to find food
in even the saltiest lakes.

Amazon rainforest

The Amazon is the Earth's largest tropical rainforest, and it surrounds one of the world's largest rivers — the Amazon River. Lots of species live here, including more than 430 mammals, 3,000 fish, 1,300 birds, 870 reptiles and amphibians, and 2.5 million insects!

A young collared anteater rides on its mother's back.

Collared anteater

This tree-climbing anteater doesn't have any teeth. Instead it slurps up ants and termites with a tongue that can be 40 cm (16 in) long!

Yellow-banded poison dart frog

This frog's bright-yellow colour tells predators to keep away. It is a serious warning, as its skin gives off toxic chemicals that can kill other animals.

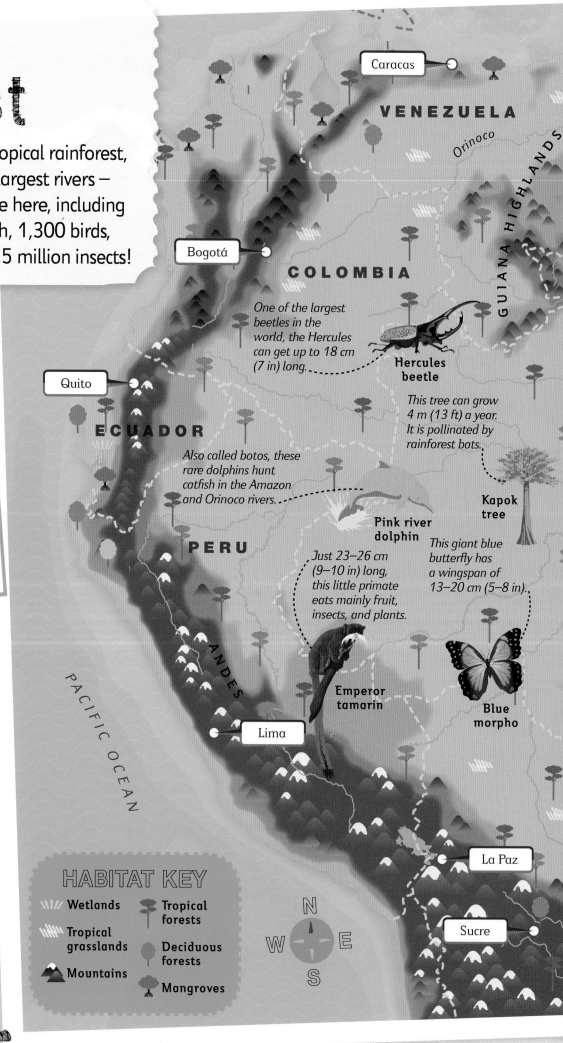

Caracas

VENEZUELA

Orinoco

GUIANA HIGHLANDS

Bogotá

COLOMBIA

One of the largest beetles in the world, the Hercules can get up to 18 cm (7 in) long.

Hercules beetle

Quito

ECUADOR

This tree can grow 4 m (13 ft) a year. It is pollinated by rainforest bats.

Also called botos, these rare dolphins hunt catfish in the Amazon and Orinoco rivers.

Kapok tree

Pink river dolphin

PERU

This giant blue butterfly has a wingspan of 13–20 cm (5–8 in).

Just 23–26 cm (9–10 in) long, this little primate eats mainly fruit, insects, and plants.

ANDES

Emperor tamarin

Blue morpho

PACIFIC OCEAN

Lima

La Paz

HABITAT KEY

||| Wetlands
|||||| Tropical grasslands
▲ Mountains
🌳 Tropical forests
🌳 Deciduous forests
🌳 Mangroves

N
W E
S

Sucre

22

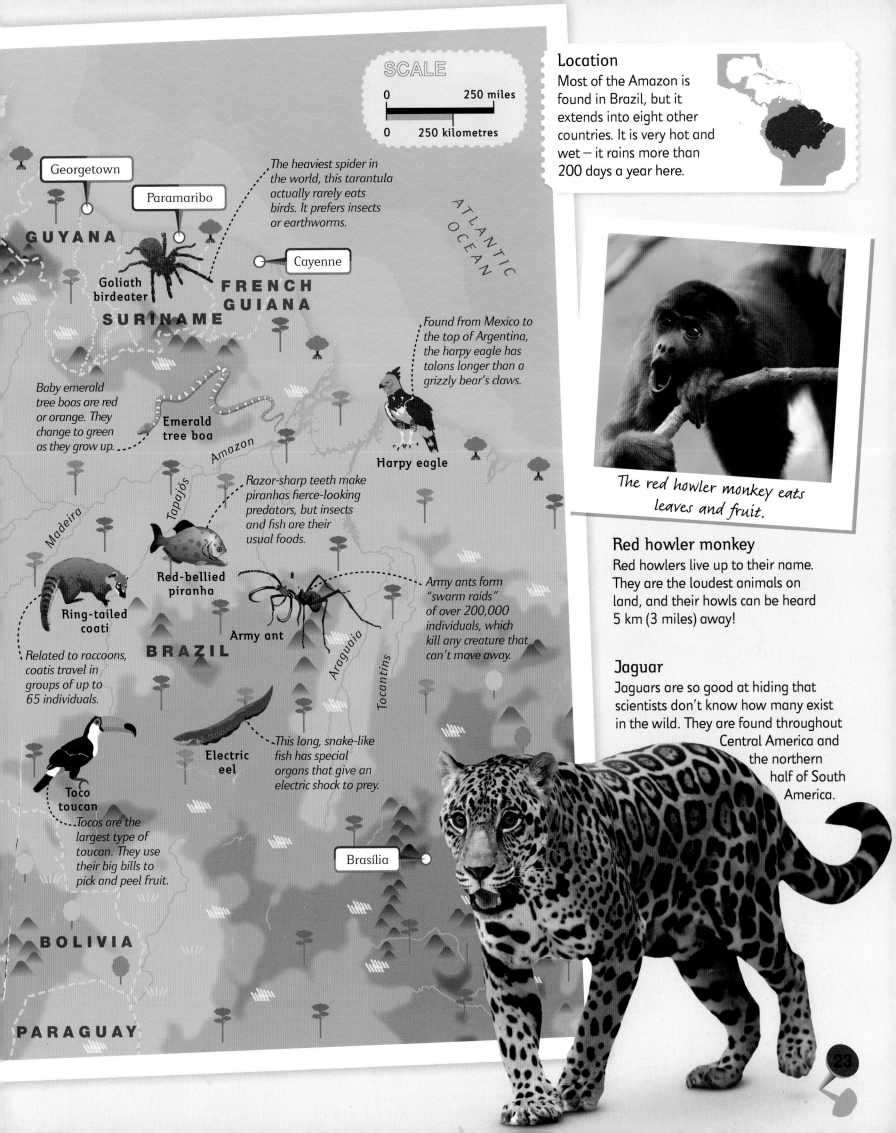

Location
Most of the Amazon is found in Brazil, but it extends into eight other countries. It is very hot and wet — it rains more than 200 days a year here.

The red howler monkey eats leaves and fruit.

Red howler monkey
Red howlers live up to their name. They are the loudest animals on land, and their howls can be heard 5 km (3 miles) away!

Jaguar
Jaguars are so good at hiding that scientists don't know how many exist in the wild. They are found throughout Central America and the northern half of South America.

Georgetown

Paramaribo

The heaviest spider in the world, this tarantula actually rarely eats birds. It prefers insects or earthworms.

GUYANA

Cayenne

FRENCH GUIANA

Goliath birdeater

SURINAME

Found from Mexico to the top of Argentina, the harpy eagle has talons longer than a grizzly bear's claws.

Baby emerald tree boas are red or orange. They change to green as they grow up.

Emerald tree boa

Amazon

Harpy eagle

Tapajós

Razor-sharp teeth make piranhas fierce-looking predators, but insects and fish are their usual foods.

Madeira

Red-bellied piranha

Army ants form "swarm raids" of over 200,000 individuals, which kill any creature that can't move away.

Ring-tailed coati

Army ant

Araguaia

Tocantins

Related to raccoons, coatis travel in groups of up to 65 individuals.

BRAZIL

This long, snake-like fish has special organs that give an electric shock to prey.

Electric eel

Toco toucan

Tocos are the largest type of toucan. They use their big bills to pick and peel fruit.

Brasília

BOLIVIA

PARAGUAY

SCALE

0   250 miles

0   250 kilometres

ATLANTIC OCEAN

23

Andean mountains

The Andes is one of the highest mountain ranges in the world. It reaches a top height of 6,959 m (22,831 ft) and stretches along the west coast of South America. Animals here have to cope with extreme habitats, from glaciers to tropical forests.

The Peruvian firestick eats ferns.

Peruvian firestick

The bright-red colour of this stick insect warns predators to stay away. If threatened, it releases a nasty-smelling liquid.

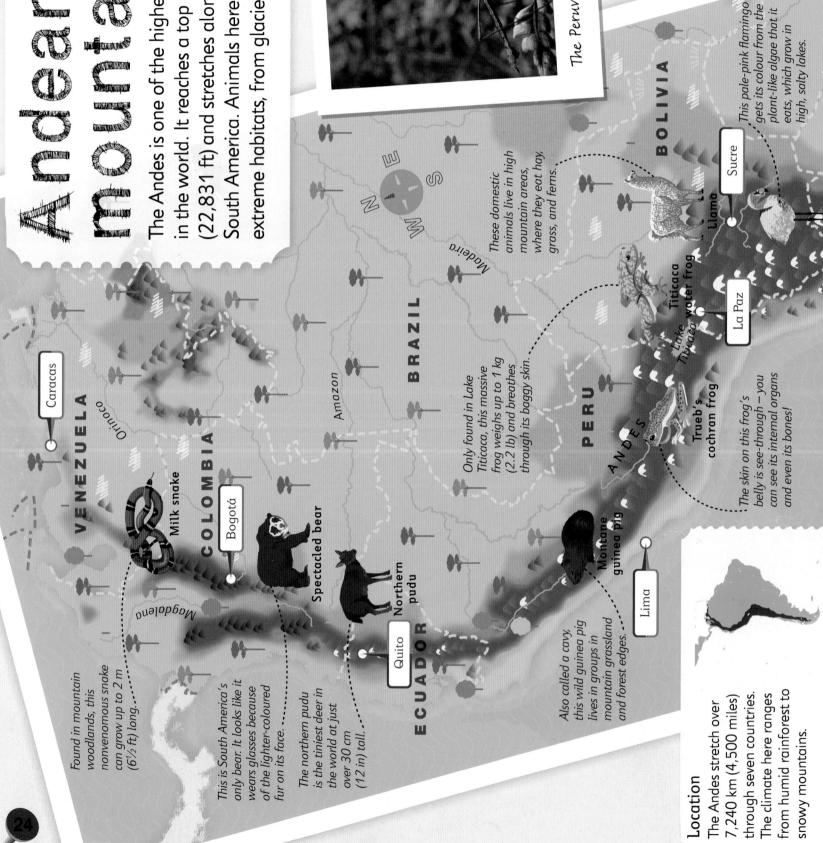

VENEZUELA

Caracas

Orinoco

COLOMBIA

Bogotá

Magdalena

Milk snake

Found in mountain woodlands, this nonvenomous snake can grow up to 2 m (6½ ft) long.

Spectacled bear

This is South America's only bear. It looks like it wears glasses because of the lighter-coloured fur on its face.

Northern pudu

The northern pudu is the tiniest deer in the world at just over 30 cm (12 in) tall.

ECUADOR

Quito

BRAZIL

Amazon

Madeira

Montane guinea pig

Also called a cavy, this wild guinea pig lives in groups in mountain grassland and forest edges.

PERU

Lima

ANDES

Trueb's cochran frog

The skin on this frog's belly is see-through – you can see its internal organs and even its bones!

Only found in Lake Titicaca, this massive frog weighs up to 1 kg (2.2 lb) and breathes through its baggy skin.

Lake Titicaca

Titicaca water frog

These domestic animals live in high mountain areas, where they eat hay, grass, and ferns.

Llama

La Paz

BOLIVIA

Sucre

James's flamingo

This pale-pink flamingo gets its colour from the plant-like algae that it eats, which grow in high, salty lakes.

N
W E
S

Location

The Andes stretch over 7,240 km (4,500 miles) through seven countries. The climate here ranges from humid rainforest to snowy mountains.

HABITAT KEY

- ╱╱ Wetlands
- ● Deciduous forests
- ╱╱ Scrublands
- ▲ Mountains
- ╱╱ Temperate grasslands
- ╱╱ Cold desert
- ╱╱ Tropical grasslands

ARGENTINA

CHILE

A N D E S

Santiago

Colorado

Negro

Chubut

SOUTH ATLANTIC OCEAN

Falkland Islands

PACIFIC OCEAN

Long-tailed chinchilla
With 60 hairs growing out of each follicle, this rodent has very thick fur. Having thick fur is ideal for the cold temperatures of the high Andes.

Mountain caracara
Caracaras often wander about, turning over stones to look for insects, rodents, and other animals to eat.

Andean goose
This goose's blood absorbs more oxygen than other geese, so it can survive at high altitudes where there is less oxygen in the air.

Andean condor
The Andean condor is the world's largest flying bird. It rides mountain air currents with a wingspan of up to 3.2 m (10½ ft).

Huemul
Short legs allow this endangered deer to clamber over rough, high mountain terrain. It is the national animal of Chile.

Culpeo
Also known as the zorro, these fox-like wild dogs hunt lizards, insects, rabbits, and geese. They make their dens in rocky caves.

SCALE
```
0        250 miles
0        250 kilometres
```

The male cock-of-the-rock can extend the crest on its head.

Andean cock-of-the-rock
Male cock-of-the-rocks are brilliant orange, while females are brownish. The males gather together to show off their feathers to females, who pick their favourite from the group.

Vicuña
These small members of the camel family are so well-adapted to their mountain homes that they can survive in altitudes as high as 5,000 m (16,404 ft).

Temperate pampas

With level plains as far as the eye can see, it's no wonder native South Americans named this region pampas — meaning "flat surface". This temperate grassland provides plenty of seeds for birds, insects, and small mammals to eat.

Eyes high on its head allow the coypu to see while swimming.

Coypu

Sometimes mistaken for a beaver, the coypu is a water-loving rodent that can get up to 1 m (3 ft) long. Also called the "nutria", it lives in riverside burrows and eats plants.

Argentine horned frog

At 14 cm (5½ in) long and weighing up to 480 g (1 lb), the horned frog is big enough to eat lizards, mice, and even other horned frogs!

This lizard gets up to 1.4 m (4½ ft) long. During the day it hunts for snails, spiders, and insects.

Argentine black and white tegu

SIERRAS DE CÓRDOBA

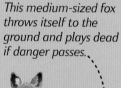

This blood-sucking bug feeds on rodents, marsupials, and even humans. It sometimes passes on a parasite that causes disease.

Assassin bug

Desaguadero

This medium-sized fox throws itself to the ground and plays dead if danger passes.

Mollina's hog-nosed skunk

This skunk uses its broad, fleshy nose to snuffle out beetles and spiders to eat.

Pampas fox

ARGENTINA

With yellow, white, green, blue, red, and black feathers, this is one of the most colourful birds to live in the reed beds of the pampas.

Many-coloured rush-tyrant

The greater rhea can reach 1.4 m (4½ ft) tall. It can't fly, but it can run as fast as 60 kph (37 mph).

Greater rhea

The long, powerful legs of this large rodent allow it to run up to 48 kph (30 mph).

Patagonian mara

Colorado

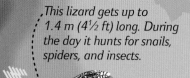

Temperate grasslands

Tropical grasslands

Wetlands

Mountains

The kingfisher plunges head-first into streams and rivers to catch small fish.

Amazon kingfisher

Salado

Paraná

N
W E
S

URUGUAY

Related to polecats and wolverines, the feisty lesser grison is excellent at hunting rabbits.

Lesser grison

Buenos Aires

Montevideo

RÍO DE LA PLATA

About the size of a domestic cat, Geoffroy's cat hunts for rodents and birds, as well as frogs and fish.

Geoffroy's cat

Pampas grass can grow up to 2.6 m (8½ ft) tall! The "plumes" on top are its flowers.

Pampas grass

Millions of these deer once roamed the pampas, but today they have to compete with cattle and humans for space.

Pampas deer

This large rodent has thick, soft fur. Several live together in enormous underground burrows.

Plains viscachas

ATLANTIC OCEAN

The male pampas meadowlark's chest is brightly coloured.

Pampas meadowlark

This endangered pampas bird likes to nest on the ground in groups. More than 60 nests have been found in one area, all clustered together.

Burrowing owl

The burrowing owl usually lives in abandoned burrows dug by other animals. It piles mammal dung around the entrance to attract dung beetles, which are one of its favourite foods.

Location

The pampas lies mainly in Argentina, stretching into Uruguay. Although it is warm and humid here, the summer dry season often brings wildfires.

SCALE

0   100 miles

0   100 kilometres

27

Pantanal

The Pantanal is the world's largest wetland, which means a lot of it is underwater for much of the year. The 3,500 different plant species that grow here make it an ideal home for lots of birds and mammals, including the capybara, which is a giant relative of the guinea pig.

Jabiru stork
The jabiru is the tallest flying bird in South and Central America, and can grow to over 1 m (3 ft) high. It grabs fish, frogs, and insects with its enormous bill.

A jabiru stork wades through the Pantanal.

This big freshwater snail grows up to 15 cm (6 in) long! It only comes out of the water at night to find food.

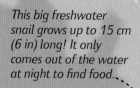

Channeled apple snail

About as big as a medium-sized dog, the capybara is the world's largest rodent.

Capybara

The roseate spoonbill sweeps its spoon-shaped bill from side to side to scoop up minnows — tiny freshwater fish.

HABITAT KEY
Tropical grasslands

Deciduous forests

Wetlands

Anacondas live in and out of water. They can be up to 9 m (29½ ft) long, but hide among water plants to surprise prey.

Green anaconda

BOLIVIA

SCALE

0   50 miles

0   50 kilometres

This wetland plant's leaves can grow to 2.5 m (8 ft) across, and can hold an animal that weighs up to 20.5 kg (45 lb)!

BRAZIL

The marsh deer has broad hooves that spread out to prevent them from sinking in marshy ground.

Marsh deer

Roseate spoonbill

Location
The Pantanal lies south of the Amazon rainforest in Brazil, Bolivia, and Paraguay. It gets so much rain that 80 per cent of it is flooded during the rainy season.

This clever monkey uses rocks to crack nuts and crush crab shells to get at the food inside.

Giant water lily

Hooded capuchin

PARAGUAY

Giant otter
Found only in South American rivers and rainforests, giant otters get up to 1.4 m (4½ ft) long. They eat fish, crabs, and even small caimans!

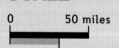

Yacare caiman
Caiman look like their alligator relatives, but have a pointier snout. The yacare gets up to 3 m (10 ft) long. Its favourite food is the piranha, but it also eats apple snails.

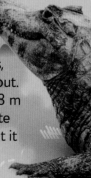

Darwin Island

Wolf Island

Galápagos

The Galápagos are a group of volcanic islands that lie around 1,000 km (621 miles) off the coast of Ecuador. There are several larger islands and many more smaller ones. Three major ocean currents meet here, bringing in lots of different sea animals.

Location
The Galápagos islands cluster around the equator in the Pacific Ocean. They have two seasons – a cool, dry season and a warm season.

PACIFIC OCEAN

Marchena Island

More lava lizards live in the Galápagos than any other reptile. They warm themselves on sunny rocks.

Although it can't fly, this cormorant is a powerful swimmer and hunts eels and octopuses on the ocean floor.

Galápagos lava lizard

Bright-blue feet make this bird easy to spot. Female boobies have darker-blue feet than males.

A marine iguana grazes on seaweed.

Marine iguana
Marine iguanas are the only lizards to swim in the sea, where they look for seaweed to eat. Special glands clean salt from their blood, which they sneeze out!

San Salvador Island

Blue-footed booby

Flightless cormorant

Fernandina Island

Galápagos hawk

Santa Cruz Island

Galápagos sea lion

San Cristóbal Island

Galápagos tortoise

This little penguin lives further north than any other penguin species.

Galápagos penguin

Isabela Island

The Galápagos hawk is very rare. It mainly eats giant centipedes, but also catches rodents and young iguanas.

This sea lion can move its back flippers independently, so it can "gallop" on land.

This tortoise can get up to 1.5 m (5 ft) long and weigh up to 227 kg (500 lb). Some of them are over 100 years old!

Sally Lightfoot crab
This bright-red crab earned its name by scuttling around at high speeds. It hides from birds by squeezing into tiny spaces between rocks.

Santa María Island

Española Island

N
W E
S

SCALE
0 ———— 25 miles

0 ———— 25 kilometres

Cerrado

The Cerrado is found almost entirely in Brazil. It is made up mainly of tropical grassland, but a few trees are mixed with it in places, and there are areas of dry forest, too. With more than 10,000 different plant species, the Cerrado offers plenty of food and shelter for lots of animals.

BRAZIL

HABITAT KEY

〜 Wetlands   Tropical forests

Tropical grasslands   Deciduous forests

Mountains   Cold desert

N W E S

Tapajós

Xing...

Both male and female hyacinth macaws are bright blue.

Hyacinth macaw

The longest parrot on the planet, the hyacinth macaw can be 1 m (3 ft) long. Their large bills are able to crack even the hardest palm nuts.

Often called "a fox on stilts", the maned wolf's long legs help it to see over the tall Cerrado grass.

The giant anteater uses its sticky tongue to lap up 35,000 ants and termites a day!

Maned wolf

Giant anteater

King vultures don't have a great sense of smell. To make up for it, they follow other vultures to lead them to dead animals to eat.

King vulture

Boettger's caecilian

BOLIVIA

Although it has no legs, this isn't a snake, but an amphibian that lives underground.

Only the male helmeted manakin has this flashy red crest. The female is a plain grey-green bird.

Helmeted manakin

Found all over Central America and the north of South America, this lizard spends most of its life in trees, where it eats tender green leaves.

Green iguana

Leafcutter ants

These ants "saw" leaves into pieces with their jaws. They carry the bits back to their underground home, where a fungus grows on them, which the ants harvest and eat.

PARAGUAY

This cat can leap up to 2 m (6½ ft) off the ground to catch birds.

Araguaia

Tocantins

Jaguarundi

Also called the racerunner, this lizard relies on speed to escape predators in the grasslands.

Giant ameiva

This bird can run at 40 kph (25 mph) for short distances – about as fast as a top human sprinter.

Sobradinho dam

The giant armadillo can grow to 1 m (3 ft) long. It rips open termite mounds with its front claws to reach the tasty insects inside.

Giant armadillo

Red-legged seriema

São Francisco

This mound houses a termite colony.

Brasília

Karimi's fat-tailed mouse opossum

Just 9.5 cm (3½ in) long, this tiny opossum stores fat in its tail like a camel stores fat in its hump.

Termites
Termites are ant-sized insects that build their own "cities". These huge mounds get up to 77 cm (30½ in) high. The mounds have underground chambers where workers store wood, care for eggs, and even grow fungal gardens for food!

Cuyaba dwarf frog

This tiny frog puffs up the two "eyespots" above its back legs to scare away predators.

BRAZILIAN HIGHLANDS

Soldier termites protect the mound with their huge jaws.

Paraná

Bush dog

ATLANTIC OCEAN

This short-legged, stocky carnivore has webbed feet, which make it a good swimmer.

Worker termites are smaller than soldiers and don't have large jaws.

Cordillera Blanca

Part of the Andes, this is the largest tropical mountain range in the world. Peaks over 6,000 m (19,685 ft) high surround valleys filled with lakes and streams. There isn't much oxygen at these heights, so it is hard to breathe, but the animals here cope surprisingly well.

Andean condor Female condors produce just one egg every two years. It takes almost 60 days for the egg to hatch.

Taruca

You can tell a taruca apart from other deer by the dark, Y-shaped mark on its face. It feeds on mountain grasses, and travels into valleys to find water.

Guanaco The guanaco is a member of the camel family. Movable pads on its hooves help it walk over rocky ground.

The guanaco is the ancestor of domestic llamas. The closely related vicuña is the ancestor of domestic alpacas.

Andean goose The Andean goose lives in mountain wetlands, but it doesn't swim well, so it avoids the water!

Colocolo The colocolo is a nocturnal predator that hunts rodents, guinea pigs, and ground-nesting birds.

Viscachas are related to chinchillas.

Southern mountain viscacha

The rabbit-like viscacha spends a lot of time on rocky ledges, basking in the sun. It is covered in thick, soft fur all the way to the end of its curled tail.

The colocolo resembles a house cat, but can be identified by the dark-coloured bands and lines around its legs.

Mountain caracara This black-and-white bird of prey builds nests of sticks on diff ledges in the high Andes.

Torrent duck
Native to the Andes, the torrent duck plunges in and out of cold, fast-moving mountain streams to catch insect larvae to eat. Females, like this one, are orange, but males are black and white.

The spectacled bear lives only in the Andean mountains.

Spectacled bear The spectacled bear eats fruit, flowers, and plants. It also hunts insects, rodents, and birds in grassland habitats.

Culpeo The culpeo spends most of its time alone, but parents stay together to raise cubs in mountain dens.

Location
The Cordillera Blanca is a chain of mountains in northern Peru. Snow covers many of them, and temperatures range from 3–23°C (37–73°F).

Giant hummingbird
Giant hummingbirds get up to 21.5 cm (8½ in) long! They feed mainly on nectar from flowers, looking for the ones with the highest levels of energy-filled sugar. They also eat spiders and small insects.

Giant hummingbirds are the biggest hummingbirds in the world.

Africa

This continent is so large and has so many different habitats, it feels as if there are several Africas, not just one. With deserts and rainforests, mountains and grasslands, Africa is home to some of the best-known — and most endangered — species on Earth.

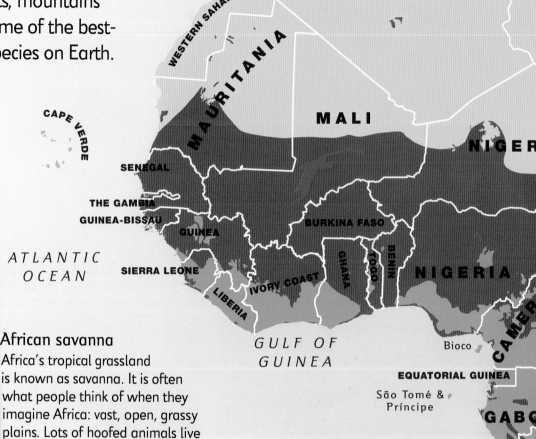

Canary Islands
(SPAIN)

MOROCCO

TUNISIA

ALGERIA

WESTERN SAHARA

MAURITANIA

MALI

NIGER

CAPE VERDE

SENEGAL

THE GAMBIA

GUINEA-BISSAU

GUINEA

BURKINA FASO

SIERRA LEONE

IVORY COAST

GHANA

TOGO

BENIN

NIGERIA

LIBERIA

ATLANTIC OCEAN

GULF OF GUINEA

Bioco

CAMEROON

EQUATORIAL GUINEA

São Tomé & Príncipe

GABON

CONGO

N W E S

African savanna
Africa's tropical grassland is known as savanna. It is often what people think of when they imagine Africa: vast, open, grassy plains. Lots of hoofed animals live here, moving around in search of fresh grass — or, in the giraffe's case, tender acacia leaves to eat.

South African fynbos
The southwest tip of South Africa is covered with shrubs and heathland known as fynbos. Animals such as tortoises, frogs, and small baboons live among the 9,000 plant species that grow here. That's more plant species than in South America's Amazon rainforest!

HABITAT KEY

Tropical forests

Deciduous forests

Coniferous forests

Tropical grasslands

Scrublands

Deserts

Wetlands

Mountains

Mangroves

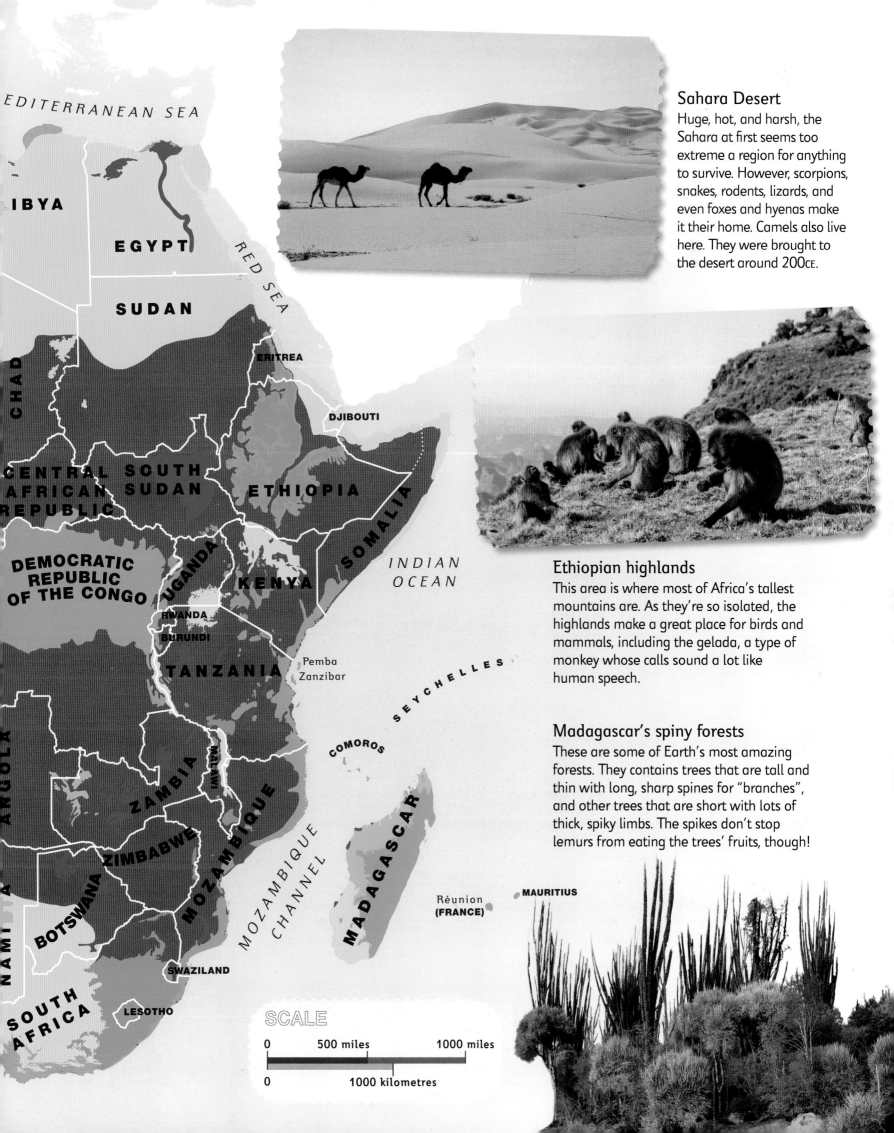

MEDITERRANEAN SEA

LIBYA

EGYPT

RED SEA

SUDAN

CHAD

ERITREA

DJIBOUTI

CENTRAL
AFRICAN
REPUBLIC

SOUTH
SUDAN

ETHIOPIA

DEMOCRATIC
REPUBLIC
OF THE CONGO

UGANDA

KENYA

SOMALIA

INDIAN
OCEAN

RWANDA

BURUNDI

TANZANIA

Pemba
Zanzibar

SEYCHELLES

ANGOLA

ZAMBIA

MALAWI

COMOROS

MOZAMBIQUE

MOZAMBIQUE
CHANNEL

MADAGASCAR

ZIMBABWE

NAMIBIA

BOTSWANA

Réunion
(FRANCE)

MAURITIUS

SWAZILAND

SOUTH
AFRICA

LESOTHO

SCALE

0   500 miles   1000 miles

0   1000 kilometres

Sahara Desert

Huge, hot, and harsh, the Sahara at first seems too extreme a region for anything to survive. However, scorpions, snakes, rodents, lizards, and even foxes and hyenas make it their home. Camels also live here. They were brought to the desert around 200CE.

Ethiopian highlands

This area is where most of Africa's tallest mountains are. As they're so isolated, the highlands make a great place for birds and mammals, including the gelada, a type of monkey whose calls sound a lot like human speech.

Madagascar's spiny forests

These are some of Earth's most amazing forests. They contains trees that are tall and thin with long, sharp spines for "branches", and other trees that are short with lots of thick, spiky limbs. The spikes don't stop lemurs from eating the trees' fruits, though!

Algiers

Rabat

MOROCCO

ATLAS MOUNTAINS

T

This is Africa's only wild sheep. Males charge at each other with their heads down when fighting.

Barbary sheep

Just 10 cm (4 in) long, this lizard licks its eyes to clean them.

Dune gecko

This snake's "horns" are really special scales that protect its eyes from sand.

Desert horned viper

Striped hyena
Also found in Asia as far as India, this night-time hunter has teeth and jaws strong enough to crush bone.

WESTERN SAHARA

Desert monitor lizard

The desert monitor uses its long, powerful tail like a whip to defend itself.

AHAGGAR MOUNTAINS

ALGERIA

ADRAR DES IFORAS

MALI

MAURITANIA

Also called a "screwhorn antelope", the endangered addax has horns up to 120 cm (47 in) long.

Addax

Gigantic swarms of desert locusts can contain billions of insects and stretch for 64 km (40 miles).

Niger

Desert locust

NIGER

ATLANTIC OCEAN

Nouakchott

SCALE

0   250 miles

0   250 kilometres

Niamey

Bamako

Sahara Desert

The Sahara is the Earth's largest hot desert. It covers 9,400,000 sq km (3,630,000 sq miles) and is home to about 70 animal and 500 plant species. They have to cope with temperatures as high as 57°C (135°F) and very little rainfall.

Abuja

Fennec fox
This small fox's huge ears aren't only great for hearing. They also help to keep the fox cool by releasing its body heat into the air.

Tunis

Tripoli

HABITAT KEY

Tropical grasslands
Scrublands
Wetlands
Mountains
Hot desert

MEDITERRANEAN SEA

N W E S

Cairo

EGYPT

This scorpion's venom is highly toxic, but it is rarely fatal to humans.

Deathstalker scorpion

LIBYA

This crocodile gets up to 6 m (20 ft) long, weighs 1,000 kg (2,205 lb), and lives up to 40 years.

The tiny hopping jerboa's hind legs are four times longer than its front ones.

Lesser Egyptian jerboa

Nile crocodile

Nile

RED SEA

AïR MOUNTAINS

TIBESTI MOUNTAINS

Sandy-coloured markings make it easy for this bird to hide from desert predators.

Found in southern desert shrubland, the Nubian bustard eats large insects, leaves, fruit, and grass seeds.

The Dorcas gazelle never has to drink. It gets all its moisture from eating flowers, leaves, and bark.

Dorcas gazelle

The largest tortoise in Africa, this reptile can weigh up to 105 kg (231 lbs).

African spurred tortoise

Chestnut-bellied sandgrouse

ERITREA

Khartoum

Asmara

Nubian bustard

SUDAN

CHAD

N'Djamena

ETHIOPIA

NIGERIA

Chari

Location
The Sahara stretches across North Africa, from the Atlantic Ocean in the west all the way to the Red Sea in the east.

Dromedary camel
Dromedaries are well suited to the desert. They can store fat in their hump as food, have thick eyelashes to keep sand out of their eyes, and can drink 182 litres (40 gallons) of water in one go!

Dromedary camels have only one hump.

37

Congo Basin

Often called "Africa's Green Heart", the Congo Basin is a huge area of land surrounding the River Congo. This supports the world's second-largest rainforest, and, together with swamps and lakes, it is a haven for hundreds of amazing animals – including bonobos and chimpanzees, the closest living relatives of humans.

Emperor scorpion

At 20 cm (8 in) long, the emperor is the largest scorpion on the planet. Surprisingly, despite its big size, its sting is not deadly for humans.

HABITAT KEY

- Wetlands
- Mangroves
- Tropical grasslands
- Tropical forests
- Mountains

SOUTH SUDAN

Juba

If one buffalo is attacked by a lion, the rest of its herd will rush to defend it.

African buffalo

Although its legs are striped like a zebra's, the secretive okapi is a close relative of the giraffe.

Okapi

One of the world's most intelligent birds, gentle African greys can learn lots of human words.

African grey parrot

UGANDA

Lake Albert

Lake Edward

Kigali

RWANDA

Congo

DEMOCRATIC REPUBLIC OF THE CONGO

Bonobo

This slender, peaceful ape eats less meat than its chimpanzee cousins and spends more time in trees.

The turaco gets its bright colours from copper, which is found in the plants it eats.

Violet turaco

CENTRAL AFRICAN REPUBLIC

Ubangi

Timid bongos have many stripes that look like light and shade, so they can hide easily in dense rainforests.

Bongo

Bangui

This big cat stashes its prey up trees to keep it out of reach of other predators.

Adult male gorillas are called "silverbacks" because of the silvery-white hair that covers their backs.

Western gorilla

CHAD

MBANG MOUNTAINS

ADAMAWA HIGHLANDS

Leopard

CAMEROON

GABON

CONGO

The mandrill has the most colourful face in the monkey world – and a bluish-purple bottom!

Mandrill

Yaoundé

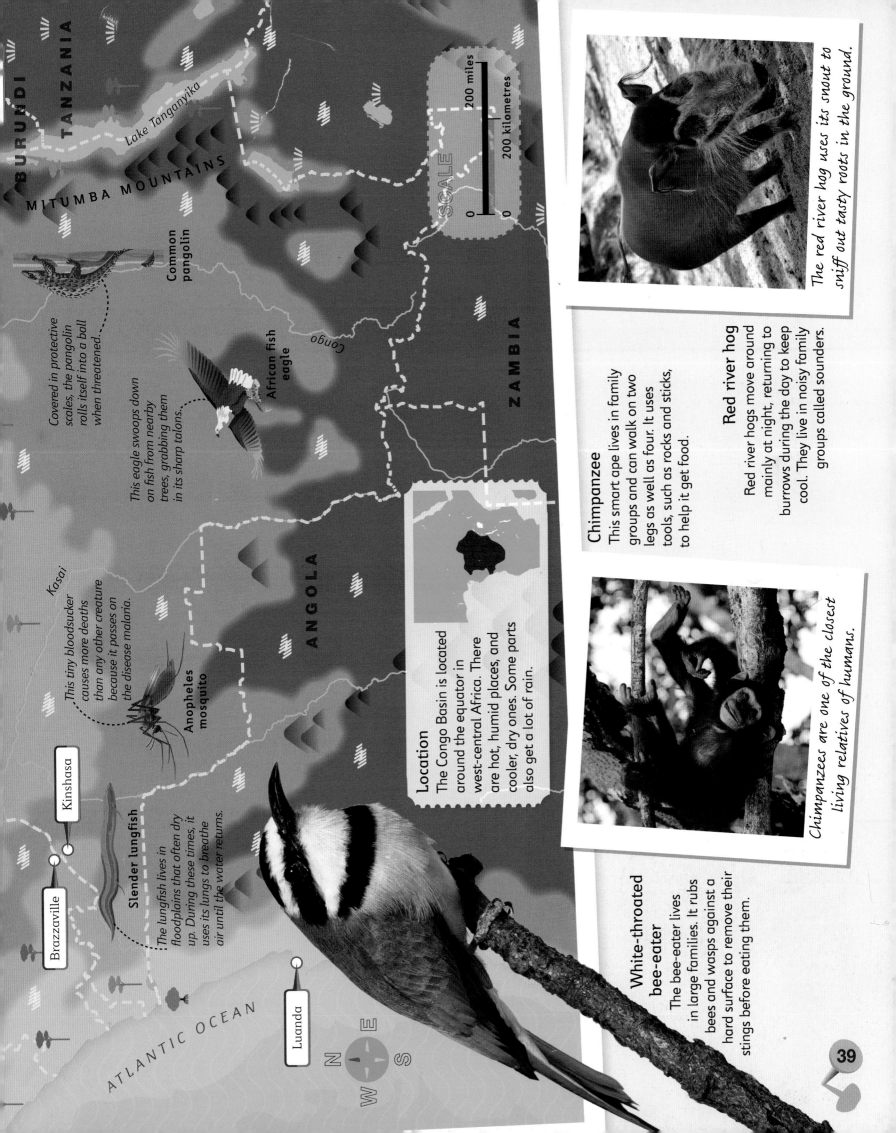

BURUNDI

TANZANIA

Lake Tanganyika

MITUMBA MOUNTAINS

Common pangolin

Covered in protective scales, the pangolin rolls itself into a ball when threatened.

African fish eagle

This eagle swoops down on fish from nearby trees, grabbing them in its sharp talons.

Congo

ZAMBIA

Kasai

This tiny bloodsucker causes more deaths than any other creature because it passes on the disease malaria.

Anopheles mosquito

SCALE

0   200 miles

0   200 kilometres

Kinshasa

Brazzaville

Slender lungfish

The lungfish lives in floodplains that often dry up. During these times, it uses its lungs to breathe air until the water returns.

ANGOLA

Location

The Congo Basin is located around the equator in west-central Africa. There are hot, humid places, and cooler, dry ones. Some parts also get a lot of rain.

Luanda

N
W   E
S

ATLANTIC OCEAN

The red river hog uses its snout to sniff out tasty roots in the ground.

Chimpanzee

This smart ape lives in family groups and can walk on two legs as well as four. It uses tools, such as rocks and sticks, to help it get food.

Red river hog

Red river hogs move around mainly at night, returning to burrows during the day to keep cool. They live in noisy family groups called sounders.

Chimpanzees are one of the closest living relatives of humans.

White-throated bee-eater

The bee-eater lives in large families. It rubs bees and wasps against a hard surface to remove their stings before eating them.

39

Southern savanna

Much of southern Africa is covered in tropical grasslands called savanna. They're great places to find grazing animals, such as zebras and antelopes. This also means that they attract predators, such as lions.

DEMOCRATIC REPUBLIC OF THE CONGO

Kinda baboon babies can have white, grey, black, or even multicoloured fur.

Kinda baboon

"Hippopotamus" means "water horse", but the hippo's closest relatives are dolphins and whales!

Hippopotamus

HABITAT KEY

- \\//| Wetlands
- \\//| Tropical grasslands
- Mangroves
- Mountains
- Deciduous forests
- Tropical forests
- Hot desert

SCALE

0   100 miles

0   100 kilometres

This tree-dwelling primate, also called a bushbaby, can jump as far as 5 m (16 ft) in a single leap.

Mohol galago

BIE PLATEAU

Zambezi

ANGOLA

Lions are sociable cats. They live in groups called prides.

African lion

African elephant

Earth's largest land animal, the African elephant has a brain four times bigger than a human brain.

These dogs help each other. They rarely fight, and they take care of young, old, sick, or injured members of their pack.

Rhinoceroses don't see very well, but they have good hearing and an excellent sense of smell.

BOTSWANA

African wild dog

Okavango

Black rhinoceros

NAMIBIA

ATLANTIC OCEAN

Grant's zebra
Just like human fingerprints, a zebra's stripe pattern is unique. This means that no two zebras have the exact same stripes.

Location
Savanna covers more than half of Africa, mainly in the central and southern parts. These areas have a rainy and a dry season, but it is hot all year.

TANZANIA

INDIAN OCEAN

MITUMBA MOUNTAINS

Lake Tanganyika

Male impalas grow beautiful ridged horns up to 92 cm (36 in) long.

Impala

Vervet monkeys spend hours each day picking dirt and parasites out of each other's fur.

MALAWI

ZAMBIA

MUCHINGA MOUNTAINS

Lake Nyasa

One of the few savanna trees, the acacia provides food for many animals – despite its fierce thorns.

Vervet monkey

Lilongwe

Acacia tree

Giraffe
At up to 5.8 m (19 ft) high, the giraffe is the world's tallest land animal. Its very long neck helps it to reach acacia tree leaves high above the savanna.

MOZAMBIQUE

Lusaka

Zambezi

Southern yellow-billed hornbill
This bird snaps up insects with its curved bill, tossing them into its mouth with a flick of its head.

INYANGA MOUNTAINS

Lesser flamingo

Long-legged flamingos sweep their bills through salty water to find algae to eat.

Harare

MOZAMBIQUE CHANNEL

N
W   E
S

Plum dung beetle
Dung beetles recycle animal poo. They roll it up into balls and bury them to use later as food or as places to lay eggs.

ZIMBABWE

Blue wildebeest
The wildebeest looks like a cow, but it is a type of antelope. It travels an astonishing 1,609 km (1,000 miles) every year, just to find the right kind of grass to eat.

Wildebeests are also known as gnus.

Kalahari Desert

The Kalahari is a huge, dry, sandy area in southern Africa. In some parts of the Kalahari, it may not rain for up to eight months. Many animals here have to travel in search of fresh grass to eat, and predators follow them.

Sociable weaver

These small birds build giant nests, over 6 m (20⅔ ft) wide, with up to 100 weavers in each one. Some nests are so heavy that they break the tree they're in!

Sociable weavers' massive nests can last for 100 years.

HABITAT KEY

\\\// Wetlands
\\\// Scrublands
\\\// Tropical grasslands
Hot desert

SCALE

0 — 100 miles
0 — 100 kilometres

Location

The Kalahari covers most of Botswana and parts of Namibia and South Africa. In summer, it can become as hot as 40°C (104°F).

ANGOLA

Okavango

Circling high in the desert sky on its broad wings, this bird searches for dead animals to eat.

White-backed vulture

Growing up to 2.8 m (9 ft) tall, the ostrich is the world's largest bird. It can't fly, but it can outrun most of its predators.

Ostrich

This high-leaping antelope moves around in large herds. Both males and females have horns.

Springbok

BOTSWANA

The aardvark's name means "earth pig". It can eat up to 50,000 ants a night!

Aardvark

Warthogs kneel on their front legs when munching on fresh grass.

 Windhoek

Common warthog

NAMIBIA

N
W — E
S

During the day, this large rodent sleeps in caves or burrows. At night, it comes out to find plants to eat.

Gaborone

Pretoria

Cape porcupine

Cheetah

The world's fastest land animal, the cheetah can run at speeds of up to 110 kph (68 mph). It takes just three seconds for this cat to reach its top speed.

African bullfrog

This big frog lives underground during the dry season, which can last 10 months of each year!

Vaal

ATLANTIC OCEAN

SOUTH AFRICA

Bloemfontein

Meerkat

Meerkats help each other protect their families. They take turns standing on guard and warn other meerkats if danger approaches.

Madagascar

Madagascar is the fourth-largest island in the world, and it is amazingly rich in wildlife. More than 250,000 different species of animals live here, and two-thirds of them are found nowhere else on Earth. Sadly, many are endangered.

43

SCALE

0 — 100 miles

0 — 100 kilometres

Location

Madagascar is in the Indian Ocean, off the coast of Africa. It has two seasons: hot and rainy, and then cool and dry.

Male panther chameleons are colour-crazy! Their body patterns are a mix of pink, blue, orange, green, red, and yellow.

Panther chameleon

MOZAMBIQUE CHANNEL

INDIAN OCEAN

Male ploughshare tortoises try to flip each other over during fights.

MADAGASCAR

Ploughshare tortoise

Betsiboka

Tomato frog

This frog's bright-red colour is a warning to predators that it is toxic.

The baobab's thick, wide trunk can hold thousands of litres of rainwater.

Lake Alaotra

Antananarivo

Leaf chameleon

Just 29 mm (1.1 in) long, this tiny species of leaf chameleon remained unknown to scientists until 2012.

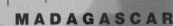

ANKARATRA MASSIF

This hedgehog-like animal has spines sticking out of its fur.

Lowland streaked tenrec

Baobab

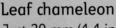

Leaf chameleons are possibly the world's smallest reptile.

HABITAT KEY

Mangroves   Tropical forests

Mountains

Deciduous forests

Mangoky

This strange-looking lemur taps its long middle finger on trees to find grubs — its favourite food.

Aye-aye

The ring-tailed lemur sunbathes every morning with its arms outstretched.

Fossa

Madagascar's largest predator is the cat-like fossa. It climbs trees and uses its long tail to help it balance. Fossas hunt many animals, from lemurs to fish.

Comet moth

The comet moth is also called the Madagascan moon moth. It has a wingspan of 20 cm (8 in) and its striking tail is 15 cm (6 in) long. This moth lives for just a few days.

Ring-tailed lemur

Kruger National Park

South Africa's Kruger National Park is filled with wildlife. More than 140 mammal species and hundreds of birds live in its savanna, mountains, and tropical forests. Watering holes provide places for animals to drink during the dry season.

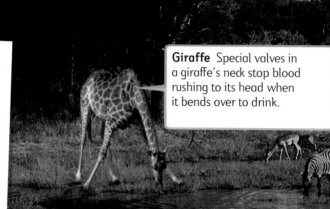

Giraffe Special valves in a giraffe's neck stop blood rushing to its head when it bends over to drink.

Hippopotamus A hippo's eyes, ears, and nose are on top of its head, so it can see, hear, and breathe while the rest of it is underwater.

Honey badger Almost 1 m (3 ft) long, the honey badger is one of the most fearless animals in Africa. It even fights lions!

Aardvark The aardvark uses its wide, strong claws to dig burrows as well as find insects to eat.

The white-backed vulture is the most commonly seen vulture in Africa.

White-backed vulture

This big vulture eats dead animals. Up to 1,000 of them may gather to feed on an elephant carcass, squabbling and fighting as they do so!

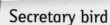

Secretary bird

The secretary bird strides through the savanna on its long legs, looking for grasshoppers, voles, and mice to eat. It kills snakes by stomping on them!

The aardvark's nostrils contain lots of hairs to stop dust going up its nose when it is digging.

Bateleur
This eagle's name means "tightrope-walker" because it rocks its wings from side to side when it glides, as if it's balancing. Its bright-red face has no feathers at all.

Plains zebra Zebra herds travel long distances to find enough grass to eat. They must also drink at least once a day.

African elephant An elephant's trunk contains 40,000 muscles! It uses its trunk to spray water into its mouth for a drink.

African elephants have much larger ears than Asian elephants.

African lion In a pride of lions, females do most of the hunting. The male is the only cat with a mane.

Impala To escape predators, impalas leap forwards up to 9 m (29½ ft) and as high as 2.5 m (8 ft). Sometimes they leap over each other!

Impalas eat grass in the rainy season and shrubs and herbs at other times.

Cheetah
A cheetah's impressive bursts of speed can only last for short distances. Afterwards, it's tired, so other animals can easily steal its kill!

Cheetahs are instantly recognizable from the black spots on their coat.

Location
Kruger National Park covers 19,485 sq km (7,523 sq miles) in northeastern South Africa. It lies south of Zimbabwe and west of Mozambique.

Europe

At first, the continent of Europe may seem too crowded for wildlife. There are 739 million people living here, in 44 countries! But with dense forests, sandy beaches, high mountains, and miles of moorland, animals still have plenty of different habitats to choose from.

Scottish moorland

Northern Scotland has acres of moorland. These rainy highlands have acidic, peaty soil, formed by sphagnum moss. They are full of a pretty pink- and purple-flowering shrub called heather. Heather is home to many insects, birds, and small mammals.

The Camargue

This triangular coastal wetland is found where the River Rhône meets the Mediterranean sea. Its 930 sq km (359 sq miles) of sandy marshes are home to 400 bird species, and to animals unique to this area, such as the Camargue horse.

HABITAT KEY

- Deciduous forests
- Coniferous forests
- Scrublands
- Temperate grasslands
- Deserts
- Tundra
- Ice

ATLANTIC OCEAN

ICELAND

Faroe Islands

Shetland Islands

NORWEGIAN SEA

NORWAY

SWEDEN

NORTH SEA

DENMARK

Bornhol

IRELAND

Isle of Man

UNITED KINGDOM

NETHERLANDS

BELGIUM

GERMANY

Channel Islands

LUXEMBOURG

CZECH REPUBLIC

BAY OF BISCAY

FRANCE

LIECHTENSTEIN

SWITZERLAND

AUSTR

SLOVE

PORTUGAL

SAN MARINO

ADRIATIC

CRO

ANDORRA

MONACO

ITALY

Corsica

SPAIN

Majorca *Minorca*

Ibiza

Sardinia

VATICAN CITY

Balearic Islands

TYRRHENIAN SEA

Gibraltar

MEDITERRANEAN SEA

Sicily

MALTA

0   500 miles   1000 miles

0   1000 kilometres

FINLAND

LTIC SEA

ESTONIA

LATVIA

LITHUANIA

RUSSIA
(KALININGRAD)

BELARUS

OLAND

UKRAINE

VAKIA

MOLDOVA

NGARY

ROMANIA

SERBIA

KOSOVO
(DISPUTED)

BULGARIA

MONTENEGRO

ALBANIA

MACEDONIA

TURKEY

GREECE

AEGEAN
SEA

IONIAN
SEA

Crete

RUSSIA
(European Russia)

Crimea

BLACK SEA

CASPIAN SEA

N
W E
S

Northern taiga

The coniferous forests of Norway, Sweden, Finland, Russia, and Iceland have long, cold winters and mild summers. Animals like the Eurasian moose prefer it that way – they overheat easily, so the cool taiga is one of their favourite places!

Mediterranean coast

Thousands of people live near the Mediterranean Sea, and there are always plenty of visitors. This leaves little space for wildlife. However, larger mammals, such as the endangered Mediterranean monk seal, are found on rocky offshore islands.

Carpathian Mountains

The Carpathian Mountains run for 1,500 km (932 miles) through Central and Eastern Europe. They are home to wolves, wild boar, and around 8,000 brown bears, mainly in Slovakia, Poland, Ukraine, and Romania.

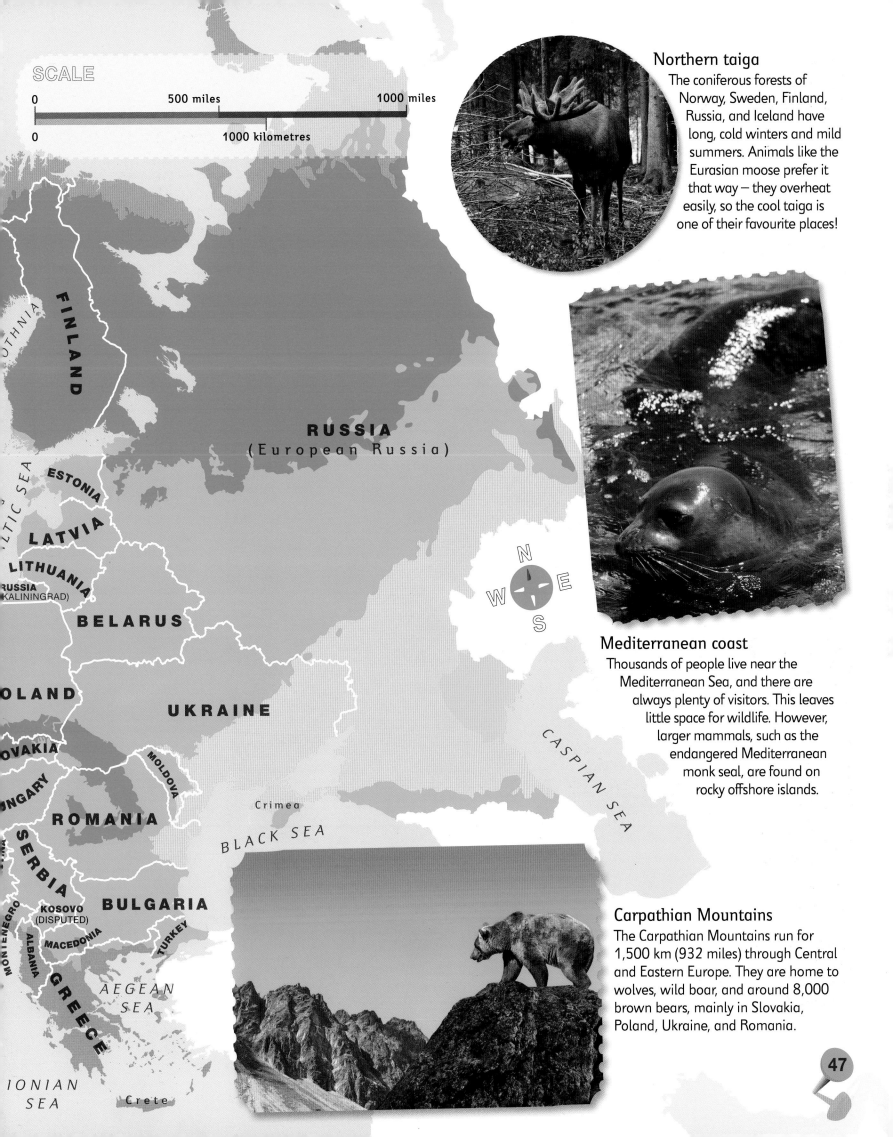

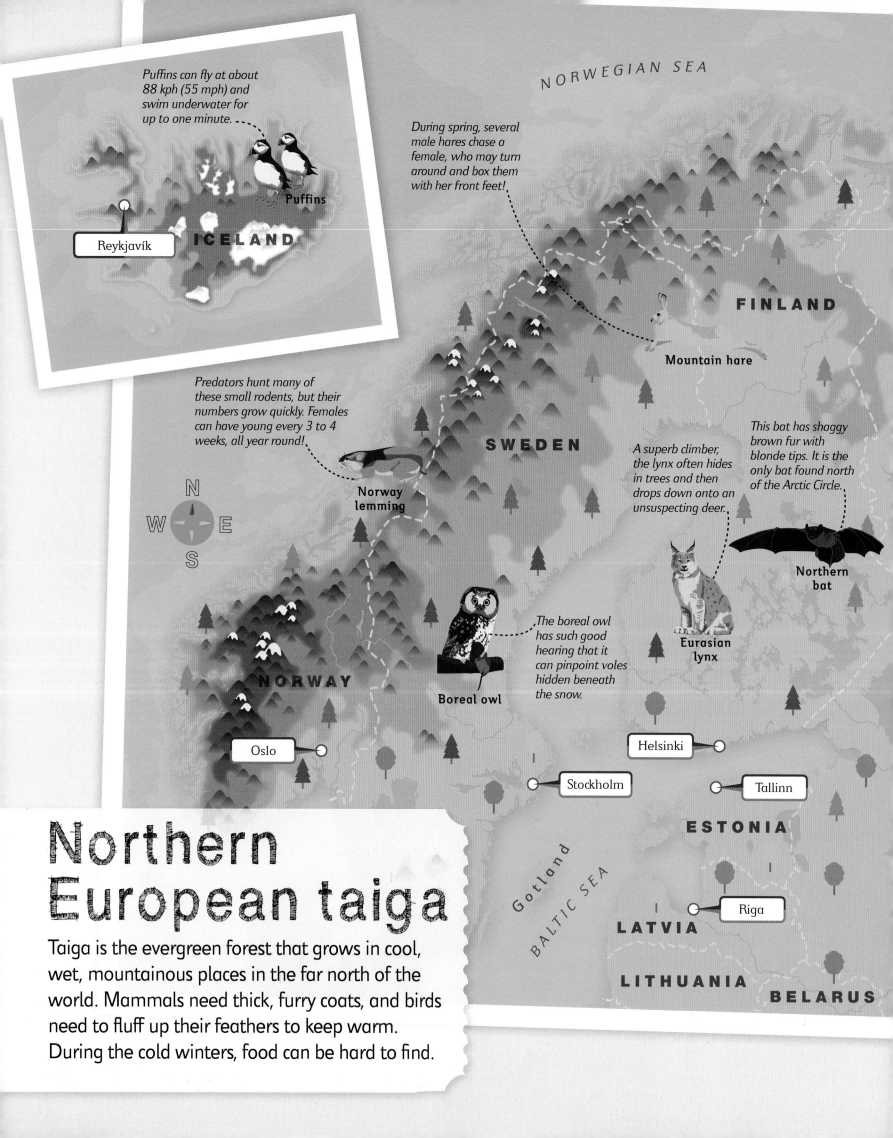

Puffins can fly at about 88 kph (55 mph) and swim underwater for up to one minute.

Puffins

Reykjavík

ICELAND

NORWEGIAN SEA

During spring, several male hares chase a female, who may turn around and box them with her front feet!

FINLAND

Mountain hare

Predators hunt many of these small rodents, but their numbers grow quickly. Females can have young every 3 to 4 weeks, all year round!

SWEDEN

This bat has shaggy brown fur with blonde tips. It is the only bat found north of the Arctic Circle.

A superb climber, the lynx often hides in trees and then drops down onto an unsuspecting deer.

N
W · E
S

Norway lemming

Northern bat

The boreal owl has such good hearing that it can pinpoint voles hidden beneath the snow.

Eurasian lynx

NORWAY

Boreal owl

Oslo

Helsinki

Stockholm

Tallinn

ESTONIA

Riga

Gotland

BALTIC SEA

LATVIA

LITHUANIA

BELARUS

Northern European taiga

Taiga is the evergreen forest that grows in cool, wet, mountainous places in the far north of the world. Mammals need thick, furry coats, and birds need to fluff up their feathers to keep warm. During the cold winters, food can be hard to find.

Carrion crow
The crow has a huge brain for its size. It's so clever that it makes and uses tools, and recognizes faces. It will even teach other crows to identify a mean human!

BARENTS SEA

This type of finch's bill is crossed at the tip, which is ideal for pulling conifer seeds out of cones.

Parrot crossbill

Used as Christmas trees, the Norway spruce can grow to 40 m (131 ft) in height and live for 1,000 years.

Also called the fish eagle, the osprey plunges into water feetfirst to grab fish with its talons.

The wolverine is the biggest member of the weasel family. It has a bite so powerful it can crush bone.

Osprey

Wolverine

The eider swallows mussels whole, crushing their shells in its stomach.

Common eider
The eider is the northern hemisphere's largest duck. Mother eiders lead their chicks to the sea, where they swim in groups of more than 150 chicks!

Norway spruce

RUSSIAN FEDERATION

Northern Dvina

The jay survives cold winters by storing food, especially berries. It hides them in trees, or covers them with bark and lichens.

Siberian jay

Lake Onega

Male capercaillies perform a dance in an area called a "lek" to attract females. They put their tails up, their wings down, and make sounds like popping corks!

Western capercaillie

Sukhoma

HABITAT KEY

▲ Mountains   ▲ Coniferous forests

● Deciduous forests

This toad's skin gives off a nasty substance that stops most predators from eating it. It can live for up to 40 years.

Common toad

Stoat
The stoat is a lightning-fast member of the weasel family. Usually reddish brown, its coat turns white in winter, making it hard to see against the snow. However, the tip of its tail stays dark.

Location
This part of the taiga runs across the top of Europe eastwards to the Ural mountains in western Russia. Winters here are very cold and snowy.

When a stoat has its white coat, it's called an ermine.

49

British Isles

The British Isles are made up of the United Kingdom – which includes England, Scotland, Wales, and Northern Ireland – and the Republic of Ireland. Although wolves and bears once lived here, today the largest wild mammal is a deer.

European badger
The badger likes to live in groups. Six or more share a system of underground tunnels called a sett, which they dig out with powerful claws. One badger can eat hundreds of earthworms in a single night!

The European hedgehog has around 5,000 spines in its coat.

European hedgehog
If threatened, this hedgehog curls up into a ball. Although it is known for eating earthworms and slugs, it actually prefers insects – even wasps and bees.

Red squirrels can be right- or left-handed – you can tell by the way they handle a pine cone.

Red squirrel

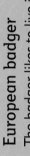

Edinburgh

This wildcat looks like a big domestic cat, but it's really a fierce, strong predator with 18 razor-sharp claws!

Scottish wildcat

Cold British waters don't bother this marine mammal. It has a 6 cm (2½ in) layer of fat under its skin, called blubber, to keep it warm.

Grey seal

Shetland Islands

Orkney Islands

Inner Hebrides

Outer Hebrides

GRAMPIANS

Clyde

Scotland

NORTH SEA

ATLANTIC OCEAN

Location
This group of islands is found off the northwest coast of mainland Europe. The weather is often wet and windy, but summers can also be very warm.

SCALE
0   50 miles
0   50 kilometres

N E S W

HABITAT KEY
Wetlands
Mountains
Coniferous forests
Deciduous forests

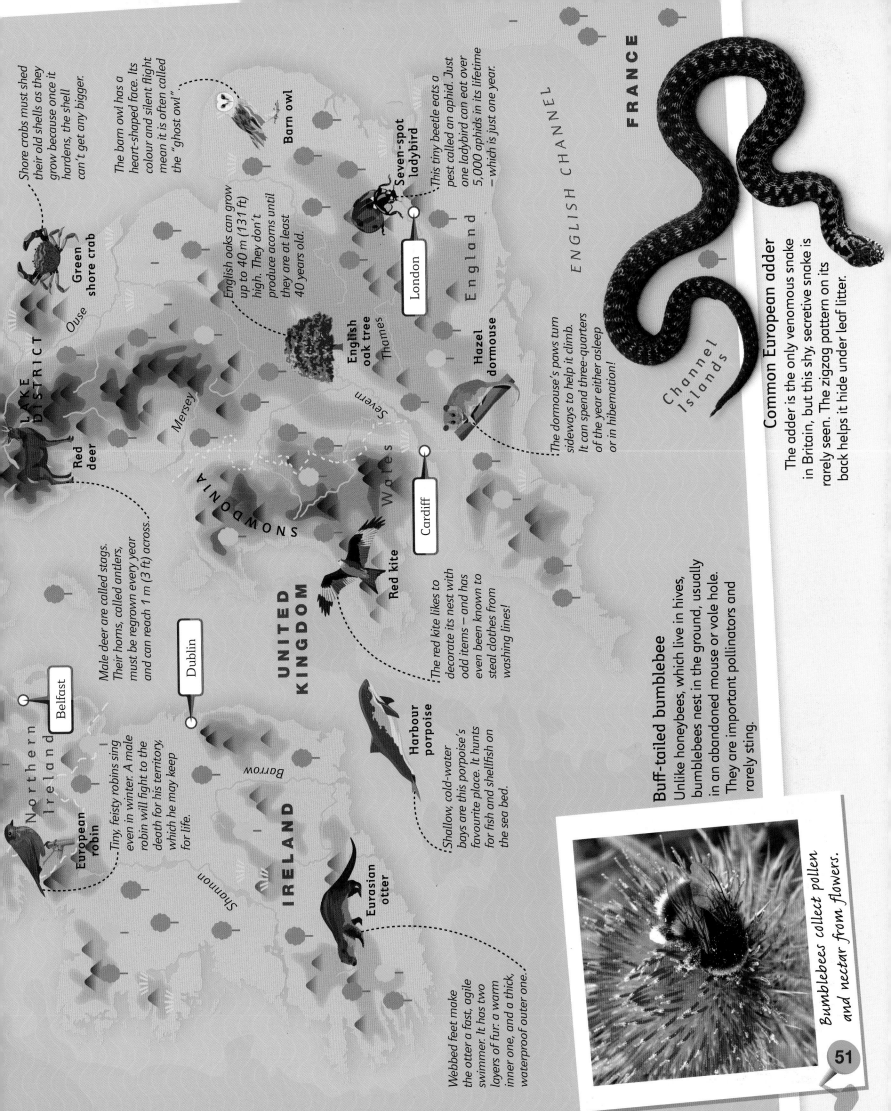

Shore crabs must shed their old shells as they grow because once it hardens, the shell can't get any bigger.

Green shore crab

The barn owl has a heart-shaped face. Its colour and silent flight mean it is often called the "ghost owl".

Ouse

Barn owl

English oaks can grow up to 40 m (131 ft) high. They don't produce acorns until they are at least 40 years old.

This tiny beetle eats a pest called an aphid. Just one ladybird can eat over 5,000 aphids in its lifetime – which is just one year.

Seven-spot ladybird

English oak tree

Thames

London

E n g l a n d

LAKE DISTRICT

Mersey

Red deer

Severn

Hazel dormouse

W a l e s

S N O W D O N I A

The dormouse's paws turn sideways to help it climb. It can spend three-quarters of the year either asleep or in hibernation!

Cardiff

Red kite

The red kite likes to decorate its nest with odd items – and has even been known to steal clothes from washing lines!

Male deer are called stags. Their horns, called antlers, must be regrown every year and can reach 1 m (3 ft) across.

U N I T E D
K I N G D O M

Dublin

N o r t h e r n
I r e l a n d

Belfast

Tiny, feisty robins sing even in winter. A male robin will fight to the death for his territory, which he may keep for life.

European robin

Barrow

Harbour porpoise

Shallow, cold-water bays are this porpoise's favourite place. It hunts for fish and shellfish on the sea bed.

I R E L A N D

Shannon

Eurasian otter

Webbed feet make the otter a fast, agile swimmer. It has two layers of fur: a warm inner one, and a thick, waterproof outer one.

E N G L I S H   C H A N N E L

FRANCE

C h a n n e l
I s l a n d s

Common European adder

The adder is the only venomous snake in Britain, but this shy, secretive snake is rarely seen. The zigzag pattern on its back helps it hide under leaf litter.

Buff-tailed bumblebee

Unlike honeybees, which live in hives, bumblebees nest in the ground, usually in an abandoned mouse or vole hole. They are important pollinators and rarely sting.

Bumblebees collect pollen and nectar from flowers.

51

European forests

Forests here mostly have a mix of trees. Some, like the Bavarian Forest in Germany, have more conifers, such as spruce. Others, such as Białoweża Forest in Poland, have more broadleaf trees, like oak. All, however, provide great homes for animals.

NORWAY

FINLAND

Oslo

Stockholm

SWEDEN

BALTIC SEA

Copenhagen

LATVIA

E

This little rodent doesn't hibernate in winter. Instead, it moves about beneath the snow, searching for plants to eat.

LITHUAN

DENMARK

Families of blue tits gather together in winter to search for food. They eat insects in the summer, but eat seeds in the winter.

GERMANY

A wood ant colony contains around 250,000 workers. This ant can spray formic acid to keep enemies away!

Bank vole

The Hague   NETHERLANDS

Amsterdam   Berlin

London

BRITISH ISLES

This millipede might look scary, but it is actually a vegetarian – it eats rotting plants.

Red wood ant

POLAND

Warsaw

This insect gets its name from the male's jaws, which look like the antlers of a male deer, or stag. Males get up to 7.5 cm (3 in) long.

Brussels

BELGIUM

LUXEMBOURG

Nightjars live in Africa in the winter, but return to Europe to nest in the spring. Their speckled feathers hide them perfectly among dead leaves.

Eurasian blue tit

Prague

CZECH REPUBLIC

Paris

Black millipede

SLOVAKIA

European nightjar

LICHTENSTEIN

Vienna

Bratislava

This mink is one of Europe's most endangered mammals. It lives near rivers and streams, and hunts mainly at night.

Bern

SWITZERLAND

AUSTRIA

Budapest

Stag beetle

FRANCE

SLOVENIA   HUNGARY

ROMANIA

Ljubljana

European mink

Zagreb

MONACO   SAN MARINO

CROATIA   SERBIA

BOSNIA & HERZEGOVINA

Belgrade

ANDORRA

Sarajevo

Pristina   Sofia

VATICAN CITY

MONTENEGRO

Podgorica   KOSOVO

Skopje

Rome   ITALY   Tirana   MACEDONIA

MEDITERRANEAN SEA

ALBANIA

GREECE

Red fox

This adaptable mammal can live almost anywhere – farms or city centres, marshes or mountaintops. It lives in more places in the world than any other carnivore.

A red fox's bushy tail is called a brush.

Location

There are areas of forest in mainland Europe from Portugal as far as Russia. Some get quite hot in summer, while others are cool all year round.

Lake Onega

Lake Ladoga

The ancient Romans thought this dormouse was very tasty – which is how it got its name.

Common woodpigeon

This pigeon lives in woodlands, parks, gardens, and even cities. Its feathers weigh more than its skeleton!

Edible dormouse

Moscow

The roe deer has a varied diet, eating everything from fungi and ferns to leaves and acorns. Baby roe deer are called kids.

Roe deer

Grass snake

The least weasel is only about 24 cm (9½ in) long.

Least weasel
Small, energetic, and deadly, the weasel hunts mice and voles in their burrows, which it often uses to make a den of its own. It even lines its nest with its prey's fur in winter.

BELARUS

RUSSIAN FEDERATION

Don

Volga

This snake has no venom. If it's threatened and can't escape, it plays dead, or releases a nasty-smelling substance from its rear end!

HABITAT KEY

Kiev

This colourful bird is named for its calls, which sound like "hoop, hoop, hoop". It spends most of its time on the ground, hunting for insects.

This wild ancestor of the domestic pig lives on every continent except Antarctica. Males can grow to 1.8 m (6 ft) long and weigh up to 300 kg (661 lb).

Common hoopoe

Wild boar

Scrublands

Temperate grasslands

Mountains

Coniferous forests

Deciduous forests

MOLDOVA

UKRAINE

Chisinau

Bucharest

N W E S

BLACK SEA

GARIA

Daubenton's bat
This "super-sleeper" hibernates for around six months of the year. It likes to roost near water in caves, abandoned mines, tunnels, or hollow trees.

Daubenton's bats use sound to find insect prey at night.

Eurasian eagle owl
This owl is one of the largest in the world – it has a wingspan of almost 2 m (6½ ft). It is so big, it can catch mammals as large as a full-grown fox or young deer!

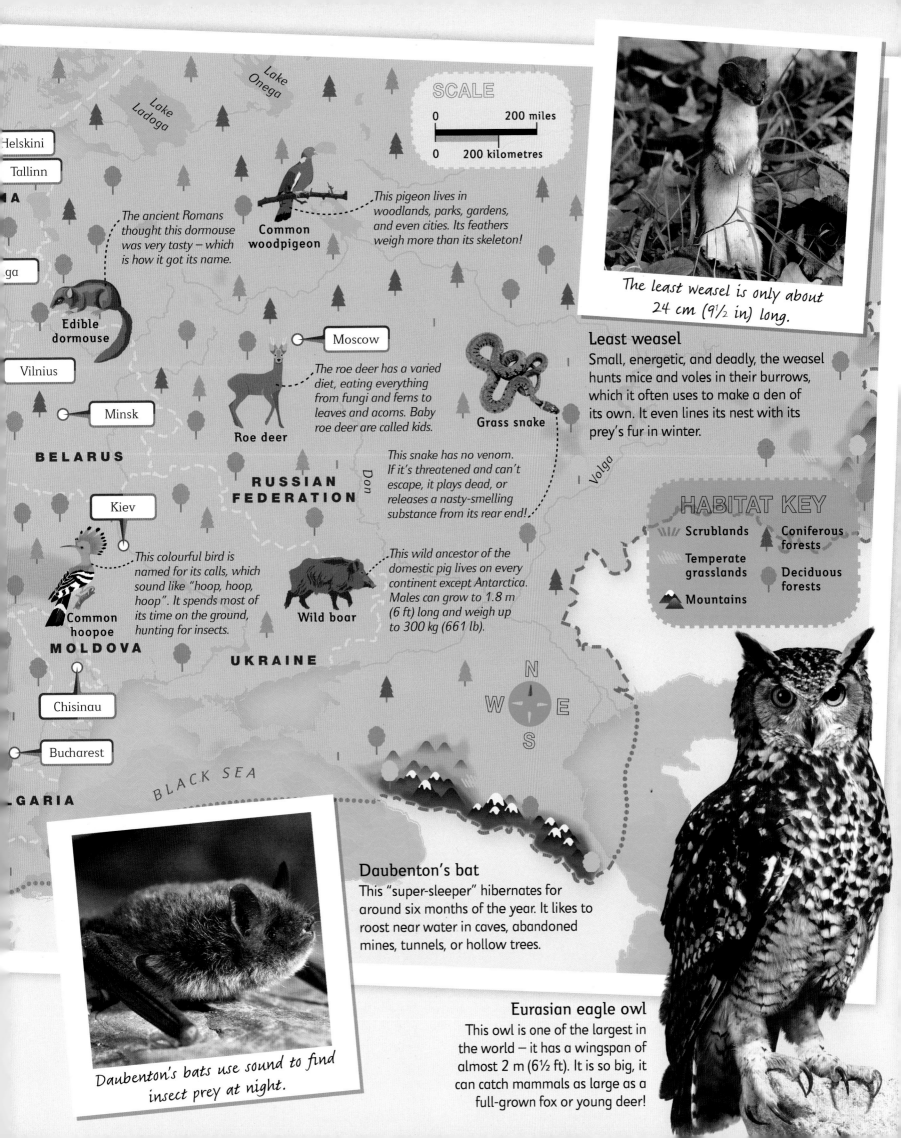

The Alps

The mountains of the Alps divide the cooler northern parts of Europe from the warm, southern parts. With mountain lakes, glaciers, meadows, and forests, there are plenty of places for different animals to live. As many as 30,000 different species make their home here.

Young shrews "caravan" behind their mother, by following each other in a line, holding on to the shrew in front by their mouth!

GERMANY

This hoofed mammal is able to run up to 50 kph (31 mph), even on a snow-covered mountain!

N W E S

LICHTENSTEIN

SWITZERLAND

AUSTRIA

Alpine shrew

FRANCE

Chamois

Bern

Rock ptarmigan

SLOVENIA

Ljubljana

This ptarmigan turns white in the winter to hide from predators in the snow.

Alpine chough

Apollo butterfly

The endangered Apollo butterfly's bright-red wing spots fade in the sun, so older butterflies have spots that are more orange.

CROATIA

Built for flight, the alpine chough has been seen soaring as high as 8,000 m (26,247 ft) above sea level!

Alpine ibex

The sure-footed ibex has long curved horns that grow up to 100 cm (39 in) long in males.

ITALY

Alpine salamander

Although it mainly comes out at night, this little black salamander also ventures out in the daytime after rain.

HABITAT KEY
Scrublands
Coniferous forests
Mountains
Deciduous forests

SCALE
0 —————— 100 miles
0 —————— 100 kilometres

Pine marten
Powerful forelimbs and strong claws make martens excellent climbers. They even race through the trees to hunt squirrels.

Alpine marmot
The alpine marmot digs long, deep burrows where it hibernates for up to nine months of the year. When hibernating, a marmot breathes just one to two times a minute!

The marmot lives in high alpine meadows and pastures.

European steppe

The steppe is a temperate grassland habitat. Many animals here are seasonal visitors from other habitats, while some, such as hamsters and moles, live here all year round.

Black-bellied hamster

This hamster digs summer and autumn burrows 50 cm (19½ in) below the ground's surface. Its winter burrow can be 2 m (6½ ft) deep. When swimming, this hamster inflates its cheek pouches to act like water wings!

Black fur on its underside gives the black-bellied hamster its name.

SCALE

0 — 200 miles
0 — 200 kilometres

RUSSIAN FEDERATION

Minsk

This pink and black starling eats locusts and other grasshoppers it finds on the steppe.

This big bird of prey can live for up to 32 years old. It makes a nest, called an eyrie, in a tall tree or on a cliff ledge.

Golden eagle

The colourful marbled polecat travels up to 1 km (0.6 miles) a night searching for food.

BELARUS

The mole's big forepaws are always turned outwards to help it dig its underground tunnels.

Kiev — **Rosy starling**

Although they each have their own burrow, there might be 6,000 giant mole rats in just 1 sq kilometre (0.4 sq miles) of grassland!

UKRAINE

Marbled polecat

HABITAT KEY

Scrublands

Coniferous forests

Mountains

European mole

Great bustard

Harvest mouse

Giant mole rat

Deciduous forests

This is the heaviest flying bird on Earth — males weigh up to 16 kg (35 lb)!

Weighing just 6 g (0.2 oz), the tiny harvest mouse is Europe's smallest rodent.

ROMANIA

Bucharest

BULGARIA

Sofia

N
W E
S

MACEDONIA

Only males have a crest on their backs.

Location

The European steppe stretches from Romania in the west to the Ural Mountains in the east, where it merges with the Asian steppe.

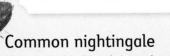

Common nightingale

This little bird is plain to look at, but its song sets it apart. Nightingale songs have high and low notes, phrases, and trills that other birds can't make.

Northern crested newt

Also called the great crested newt, this amphibian gets up to 17 cm (6½ in) long. Newts are most active at night, and spend the day hiding in ponds, or under damp logs or rocks.

Mediterranean scrubland

The coastal areas around the Mediterranean Sea contain rocky hills and flat, shrub-filled plains. This rare habitat is found in only a few places on Earth. Plants here can survive wildfires, and animals have to cope with hot, dry weather.

Mediterranean chameleon
This is one of only two chameleon species found in Europe. Its tongue is sticky to catch passing insects, and is so long that it is twice the length of its body!

This wolf is thinner and smaller than other European wolves. It hunts rabbits, deer, wild boar, birds, and fish.

FRANCE

Garonne

Rhône

MONACO

Mediterranean banded centipede

This centipede paralyzes its prey with a venomous bite and will give a human a painful nip too — so stay well away!

P Y R E N E E S

Mediterranean tree frog

Ebro

ANDORRA

SPAIN

Iberian wolf

PORTUGAL

Madrid

Tagus

Jewelled lizard

This frog is usually bright green or blue. It has suckers on its fingers and toes that let it climb with ease.

The cuckoo lays its eggs in other birds' nests. When the cuckoo chick hatches, it pushes all the other eggs out — so the parent birds feed it instead!

M a j o r c a

Sardinia Corsica

Lisbon

This monkey is found in Africa and on the island of Gibraltar, near Spain. It is the only wild monkey in Europe.

Iberian ibex

Common cuckoo

Iberian pig

The sapphire-like blue spots on its body give this lizard its name. It is the largest lizard in Europe at about 60 cm (23½ in) long.

This pig is a farmed animal, but lives in open country, looking for mushrooms, roots, and acorns from cork oaks.

Barbary macaque

A type of wild goat, male Iberian ibexes have horns that grow up to 75 cm (29½ in) long!

M E D I T E R R A N E A N   S E A

SCALE
0 — 200 miles

0 — 200 kilometres

HABITAT KEY
- Scrublands
- Wetlands
- Mountains
- Coniferous forests
- Deciduous forests

European rabbit
The European rabbit is the ancestor of all pet rabbits in the world. Unlike its enemy, the Iberian lynx, the rabbit has been seen in gardens and parks, and even in busy cities.

Location
This region includes the southern parts of Europe around the Mediterranean Sea, as well as islands like Crete that share a similar habitat.

Hummingbird hawk moth
This insect beats its wings so fast that they make a humming sound – just like the birds it's named after. It feeds on nectar made by flowers like buddleia and honeysuckle.

The hawk moth will return to a nectar-rich flower day after day.

Iberian lynx
Just 404 adult Iberian lynxes are left in the wild, so this is the most endangered cat on Earth – but the good news is this figure is nearly twice the number of wild lynxes alive a few years ago!

This cat mainly hunts just one animal – the European rabbit.

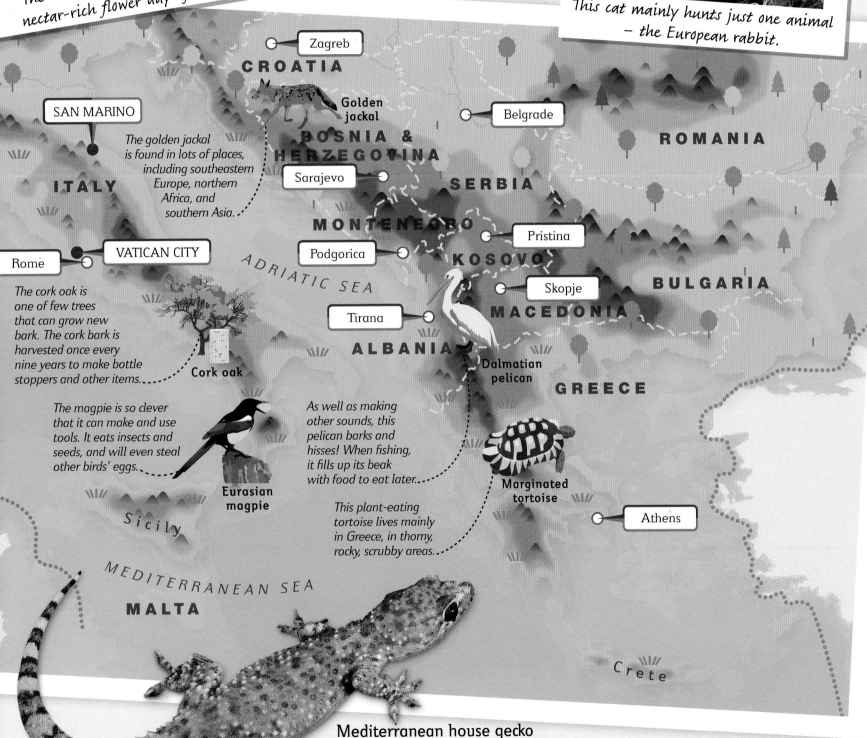

Zagreb

CROATIA

SAN MARINO

Golden jackal

The golden jackal is found in lots of places, including southeastern Europe, northern Africa, and southern Asia.

BOSNIA & HERZEGOVINA

Sarajevo

Belgrade

ROMANIA

SERBIA

ITALY

MONTENEGRO

Pristina

Podgorica

KOSOVO

Skopje

BULGARIA

VATICAN CITY

Rome

ADRIATIC SEA

Tirana

MACEDONIA

The cork oak is one of few trees that can grow new bark. The cork bark is harvested once every nine years to make bottle stoppers and other items.

Cork oak

ALBANIA

Dalmatian pelican

GREECE

The magpie is so clever that it can make and use tools. It eats insects and seeds, and will even steal other birds' eggs.

As well as making other sounds, this pelican barks and hisses! When fishing, it fills up its beak with food to eat later.

Eurasian magpie

Marginated tortoise

Sicily

This plant-eating tortoise lives mainly in Greece, in thorny, rocky, scrubby areas.

Athens

MEDITERRANEAN SEA

MALTA

Crete

Mediterranean house gecko
This little gecko is about 10 cm (4 in) long and weighs about as much as a sugar cube. It is also called a "moon lizard" because it mainly comes out at night. It eats small cockroaches and moths.

57

Białowieża Forest

Białowieża is lowland Europe's only old-growth, or "primeval", forest. Forests like this once covered all of northeastern Europe. Its many different trees and habitats mean Białowieża is home to thousands of animals, including the rare European bison!

Red deer Red deer find leaves, small twigs, and bark to eat in autumn and winter, and herbs and grasses during the summer.

Pine marten Pine martens are related to weasels but, unlike weasels, they hunt in the trees. They chase small mammals such as squirrels.

Red fox Foxes feed on a wide variety of foods. In Białowieża, they eat yellow-necked mice, hares, and the carcasses of red deer killed by wolves or lynxes.

All domestic dogs are descended from the grey wolf.

Grey wolf

The grey wolf is found in Europe, North America, and Asia. Packs of four to five wolves hunt deer, elk, wild boar, rabbits, and beavers.

Common toad

Many parts of this forest are wet, including rare places known as "spruce bog forests", where coniferous spruce trees grow in very wet ground. These habitats make a perfect home for the common toad!

A male and female red fox have a territory that they share, which is where they raise their young.

Old-growth forests have plenty of standing dead trees as well as live ones. Woodpecker nests or holes where the tree has rotted make ideal bat roosts.

Great spotted woodpecker Woodpeckers nest in holes made in tree trunks. They search for tasty insect prey in the bark.

European bison The bison is Europe's largest land mammal. There are around 900 in Białowieża forest.

Tawny owl This woodland owl hunts at night for birds, rodents, amphibians such as frogs, and bats to eat.

Noctule bat
Noctule bats nest in hollow trees. The holes must be high enough to avoid predators such as pine martens. Noctules are one of the first bats to come out at night, and hunt moths and flying ants.

Eurasian red squirrel Eurasian red squirrels like to eat seeds, especially from conifer trees.

Yellow-necked mouse This mouse prefers living in woodland, because it eats a lot of tree seeds. It is also an excellent tree-climber!

Eurasian badger Badgers are common in forests. As well as plenty of worms to eat, they find lots of hollow trees, which they use as daytime shelters.

Location
Białowieża Forest covers 1,500 sq km (579 sq miles) across Poland and Belarus. Temperatures range from -6°C (21°F) in winter to 24°C (75°F) in summer.

Eurasian beaver
The Eurasian beaver disappeared from Białowieża in the mid-19th century due to hunting. It was reintroduced in 1956. Today, they live all along the rivers, streams, and ponds throughout the forest.

Beavers produce an oily substance that keeps their fur waterproof.

59

Asia

Welcome to Earth's largest continent! Asia contains half the world's human population, but there is still a lot of land for wildlife. Habitats here include vast deserts, grassy plains, snowy mountains, and dense, green rainforests.

Savanna

This region in northern India is warm all year round. It has the highest grasslands in the world — some grow more than 3 m (10 ft) tall! The grasslands provide food for deer and rhinos, and cover for predators such as the tiger.

City wildlife

The Turkish capital of Istanbul is rich in wildlife — 337 of the country's 483 bird species, such as this seagull, live here. The city is also part of an important migration route for hundreds of thousands of storks, raptors, and water birds each year.

Arabian highlands

The Arabian highlands are made of the mountains and high plateaus that border the desert of the Arabian Peninsula, in southwest Asia. The highlands are cooler than the desert, and have more rainfall, so shrubs and grasses can grow. These plants are food for animals such as camels.

MEDITERRANEAN SEA
BLACK SEA
TURKEY
CYPRUS
GEORGIA
ARMENIA
AZERBAIJAN
LEBANON
SYRIA
ISRAEL
JORDAN
IRAQ
KUWAIT
CASPIAN SEA
IRAN
TURKMENISTAN
KAZAKHSTAN
UZBEKISTAN
KYRGYZSTAN
TAJIKISTAN
AFGHANISTAN
RED SEA
SAUDI ARABIA
BAHRAIN
QATAR
UNITED ARAB EMIRATES
PAKISTAN
NEP
YEMEN
OMAN
GULF OF ADEN
Socotra
ARABIAN SEA
INDIA
SRI LANKA
Maldives
BAY
N W E S
INDI

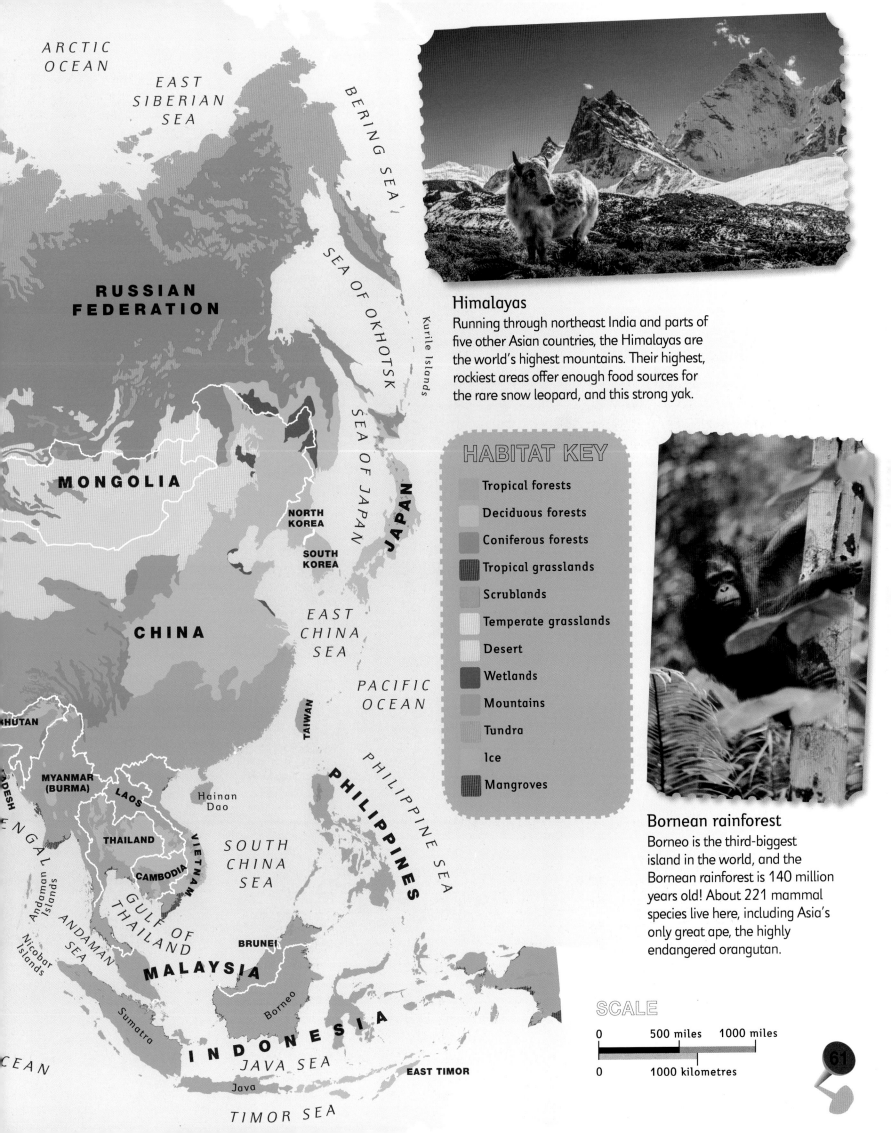

ARCTIC
OCEAN

EAST
SIBERIAN
SEA

BERING SEA

RUSSIAN
FEDERATION

SEA OF OKHOTSK

Kurile Islands

MONGOLIA

NORTH
KOREA

SEA OF JAPAN

JAPAN

SOUTH
KOREA

CHINA

EAST
CHINA
SEA

PACIFIC
OCEAN

TAIWAN

PHILIPPINE SEA

PHILIPPINES

BHUTAN

Hainan
Dao

MYANMAR
(BURMA)

LAOS

NGAL

THAILAND

VIETNAM

SOUTH
CHINA
SEA

CAMBODIA

Andaman Islands

ANDAMAN SEA

GULF OF
THAILAND

BRUNEI

Nicobar
Islands

MALAYSIA

Sumatra

Borneo

INDONESIA

JAVA SEA

Java

EAST TIMOR

CEAN

TIMOR SEA

Himalayas

Running through northeast India and parts of five other Asian countries, the Himalayas are the world's highest mountains. Their highest, rockiest areas offer enough food sources for the rare snow leopard, and this strong yak.

HABITAT KEY

Tropical forests
Deciduous forests
Coniferous forests
Tropical grasslands
Scrublands
Temperate grasslands
Desert
Wetlands
Mountains
Tundra
Ice
Mangroves

Bornean rainforest

Borneo is the third-biggest island in the world, and the Bornean rainforest is 140 million years old! About 221 mammal species live here, including Asia's only great ape, the highly endangered orangutan.

SCALE

0   500 miles   1000 miles

0   1000 kilometres

Russian taiga

Taiga is also called "snow forest". It's found in cool, high places, like in northeast Russia, and is made up of coniferous forests. Animals use trees for food and shelter, and as places to hide from predators.

KARA SEA

Fur-covered flaps of skin linking its legs let this tiny squirrel glide from tree to tree.

Siberian flying squirrel

A brown bear takes to the river to hunt for salmon.

Brown bear
The most widespread of all bear species, the brown bear mainly eats roots, berries, and other parts of plants, but it will also hunt animals. Adults can be more than 7 ft (2 m) tall when they stand on their hind legs.

The sable is a member of the weasel family. It hunts chipmunks, mice, and birds.

Sable

Ob

Irtysh

This deer has fangs! They're really tusk-like teeth that the males use to fight each other.

Siberian musk deer

Yenisei

Fast-growing birch trees shed their bark like tissue paper as they grow.

Silver birch

This wapiti is a large type of deer that forms herds of 100 or more in the autumn.

The saiga's swollen, flexible nose hangs over its mouth, helping keep out the dust kicked up by its herd in summer.

Siberian wapiti

Saiga antelope

Siberian tiger
This is the world's biggest wild cat. Males weigh up to 300 kg (660 lb). It even has a mane, like a lion's, to help keep its neck warm in cold Siberian winters.

HABITAT KEY

Wetlands

Mountains

Snow and ice

Coniferous forests

Deciduous forests

Ural owl
This big owl hunts rodents, frogs, and birds that it spots from its perch. In spring, it sings a courtship duet with its lifelong mate.

The Ural owl aggressively defends its territory, chasing away intruders.

This is the only chipmunk found outside North America. It has five dark and four white stripes running along its back.

Siberian chipmunk

Both male and female snow sheep have big, curved horns that grow in a corkscrew shape as they get older.

Snow sheep

Its main home is the taiga, but this little bird is sometimes spotted in Scotland and North America.

Siberian rubythroat

Lena

Blue robins often look for food near rivers, but they never stray far from the forest.

Siberian blue robin

N W E S

SCALE
0   300 miles
0   300 kilometres

This seal lives only in Lake Baikal, which is an icy, freshwater lake in Russian Siberia.

Baikal seal

Lake Baikal

Wood frogs spend the winter hibernating in holes in river bottoms.

Siberian wood frog

Location
Taiga stretches over northeast Russia, eastwards to the Pacific Ocean. Summers are short, but the winters are long and snowy.

Black woodpecker
Strong neck muscles and a sharp bill make this bird a champion wood-borer. It chisels out holes in tree trunks, where it lays its eggs.

Asian steppe

A steppe is a high, grassy, mostly treeless plain. Animals here live on grass and other plants — or on the animals that do! They must be able to survive freezing winters, hot summers, and harsh wind, and to go long periods without water. On the steppe, watering holes are in short supply.

Central Asian tortoise

Also called the steppe tortoise, this animal's shell is almost as wide as it is long. It has claws on each foot — and one on its tail, too!

RUSSIAN FEDERATION

This nocturnal animal can cover 18 km (11 miles) a night in its search for food.

Steppe polecat

HABITAT KEY

Wetlands

Coniferous forests

Temperate grasslands

Deciduous forests

Mountains

Cold desert

The bobak digs burrows up to 4–5 m (13–16 ft) deep, where it hibernates up to six months each year.

Bobak marmot

This wild cat's coat turns from frosty grey in winter to reddish grey in spring.

KAZAKHSTAN

Astana

SCALE

0   200 miles

0   200 kilometres

N W E S

This bird hovers above its prey before swooping down and grabbing it with its powerful talons.

This squirrel digs two types of burrows: one for hibernation, and one to hide in from predators like eagles.

Steppe eagle

Wild horses live in herds of females and foals led by a male, called a stallion. Stallions fight over who gets to lead.

Pallas's cat

Przewalski's wild horse

UZBEKISTAN

Little ground squirrel

Bishkek

CASPIAN SEA

Tashkent

Dushanbe

KYRGYZSTAN

The onager looks like a horse, but is smaller and brays like a donkey.

CHINA

TAJIKISTAN

AFGHANISTAN

Onager

Peregrine falcon

These falcons normally hunt other birds. When hunting, peregrines make a steep dive called a "stoop". During a stoop, they can reach speeds of up to 240 kph (150 mph)!

Location

The Asian steppe stretches from west of the Caspian Sea, though central Asian Russia, and as far east as the Altai Mountains.

A secret toadhead agama stands alert.

Secret toadhead agama
The insect-eating agama keeps several secrets. It may look like a regular desert lizard, but when it displays, it opens its mouth to reveal a deep reddish-pink and expands two spiny cheek flaps.

Location
There are deserts in Kazakhstan, Uzbekistan, and Turkmenistan, and parts of Afghanistan, Pakistan, and Iran.

When a predator is near, this hedgehog growls and hisses like a cat, then rolls itself into a protective ball.

Astana

The corsac fox uses its long, wide ears to listen for rodent noises in the desert.

Long-eared hedgehog

KAZAKHSTAN

Corsac fox

At up to 33 cm (13 in) long, this is the largest gerbil on Earth.

SCALE

0   200 miles

0   200 kilometres

Bishkek

This is the world's most venomous true cobra. Though it lives in the desert, it is very good at swimming.

UZBEKISTAN

Great gerbil

Tashkent

KYRGYZSTAN

N W E S

Central Asian cobra

This hare comes out at night to feed on desert plants. It rests in a shallow scrape in the ground during the day.

Yerevan

CHINA

AZERBAIJAN

TURKMENISTAN

Dushanbe

TAJIKISTAN

ARMENIA

The wild goat lives in dry, rocky areas. Its curved horns have a very sharp inside edge.

Baku

Ashgabat

Tolai hare

Tehran

Kabul

Dushanbe

Wild goat

Tehran

Islamabad

IRAN

Baghdad

AFGHANISTAN

PAKISTAN

Central Asian deserts

There are different kinds of deserts here. Some are salty and sandy. Others are rocky or have clay soil. All are dry. Water is found mainly near desert borders where rivers can overflow.

Goitered gazelle

A big, swollen tube on its throat gives this gazelle its name. It also gives males an extra-loud voice.

HABITAT KEY
- Wetlands
- Coniferous forests
- Temperate grasslands
- Deciduous forests
- Mountains
- Cold desert
- Tropical forests
- Hot desert

Tibetan Plateau

This high, flat region of Asia is surrounded by mountains. It's so high that it's often called the "roof of the world". The animals that live here have to cope with thin air and bitter winters.

Location
This region includes Tibet and parts of southwest China. Summers are dry and warm, and winters are often below freezing.

Asiatic black bear
This bear is also called the "moon bear" due to the pale, crescent-shaped band on its chest. It spends about half of its life up in trees.

Many kinds of plants grow on the plateau, including this serratula, a type of thistle.

Himalayan alpine serratula

This large, cow-like animal has extra-big lungs that help it to get enough oxygen from the thin air.

Wild yak

This little relative of the rabbit is so suited to rocky ground that it often nests in a heap of stones!

Himalayan mouse hare

PAKISTAN

The tahr is a wild goat that has hooves with rubberlike cores. These help it to grip onto smooth rocks.

Himalayan tahr

HIMALAYAS

NEPAL

INDIA

N W E S

Himalayan wolf

The Himalayan wolf is a rare type of grey wolf. Some are almost white — like snow on the Himalayas!

Himalayan marmots dig very deep burrows to hibernate in.

Himalayan marmot
Nicknamed the "Tibetan snow pig", this ground squirrel is one of the only mammals on Earth that lives above 5,000 m (16,400 ft).

When threatened, the mountain weasel scares away predators with a foul-smelling spray called musk.

Mountain weasel

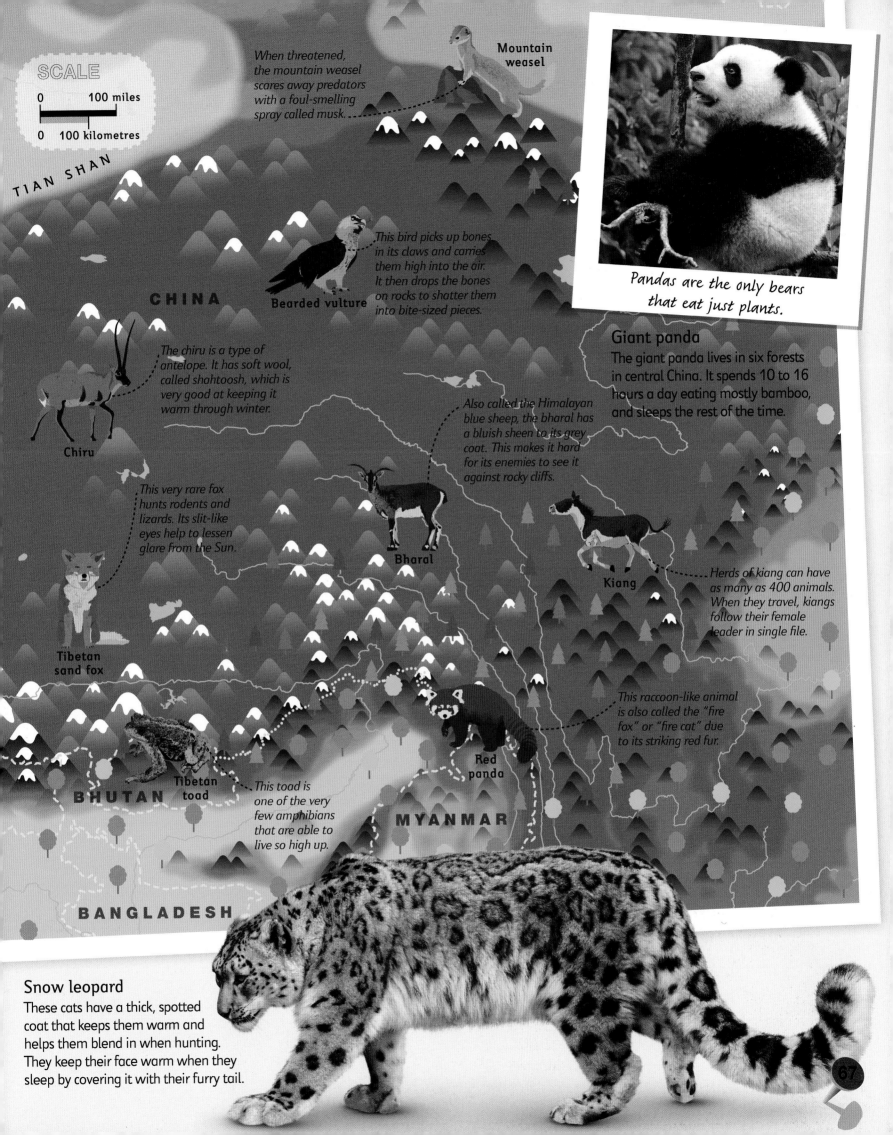

Pandas are the only bears that eat just plants.

TIAN SHAN

This bird picks up bones in its claws and carries them high into the air. It then drops the bones on rocks to shatter them into bite-sized pieces.

CHINA

Bearded vulture

Giant panda
The giant panda lives in six forests in central China. It spends 10 to 16 hours a day eating mostly bamboo, and sleeps the rest of the time.

The chiru is a type of antelope. It has soft wool, called shahtoosh, which is very good at keeping it warm through winter.

Chiru

Also called the Himalayan blue sheep, the bharal has a bluish sheen to its grey coat. This makes it hard for its enemies to see it against rocky cliffs.

This very rare fox hunts rodents and lizards. Its slit-like eyes help to lessen glare from the Sun.

Bharal

Kiang

Herds of kiang can have as many as 400 animals. When they travel, kiangs follow their female leader in single file.

Tibetan sand fox

Red panda

This raccoon-like animal is also called the "fire fox" or "fire cat" due to its striking red fur.

BHUTAN   Tibetan toad

This toad is one of the very few amphibians that are able to live so high up.

MYANMAR

BANGLADESH

Snow leopard
These cats have a thick, spotted coat that keeps them warm and helps them blend in when hunting. They keep their face warm when they sleep by covering it with their furry tail.

67

East Asian forests

Eastern Asia's deciduous forests are full of trees like oak and ash, as well as some walnut and birch. With streams and rivers, mountains and grassland edges, they are a haven for animals.

Ulan Bator

YABLONOI MOUNTAINS

MONGOLIA

GOBI DESERT

Beijing

A Chinese peacock butterfly feeds on a spider lily plant.

Chinese peacock butterfly
This forest butterfly's size depends on what time of the year it comes out of its cocoon. Spring Chinese peacocks have a wingspan of up to 8 cm (3 in). Summer ones have a wingspan up to 12 cm (5 in).

This snake eats poisonous toads, absorbs the poisons, then releases them later from its neck glands!

Asian tiger keelback

Japanese sika deer
The sika is a small deer — males are only 95 cm (3 ft) at shoulder height. They make strange noises, too, such as the male's long, whistle-like call that sounds like a siren.

This monkey has a blue face! It spends 95 per cent of its time in the trees.

Golden snub-nosed monkey

Huang He

Male Baikal teals make a deep chuckling sound — wot-wot-wot!

Baikal teal

Earth's largest amphibian grows to 1.8 m (6 ft) long. That's longer than many adult humans are tall!

Yangtze

CHINA

Chinese giant salamander

This is the smallest of the "big cats". Cloud-like spots help this leopard to blend in with its forest home.

Clouded leopard

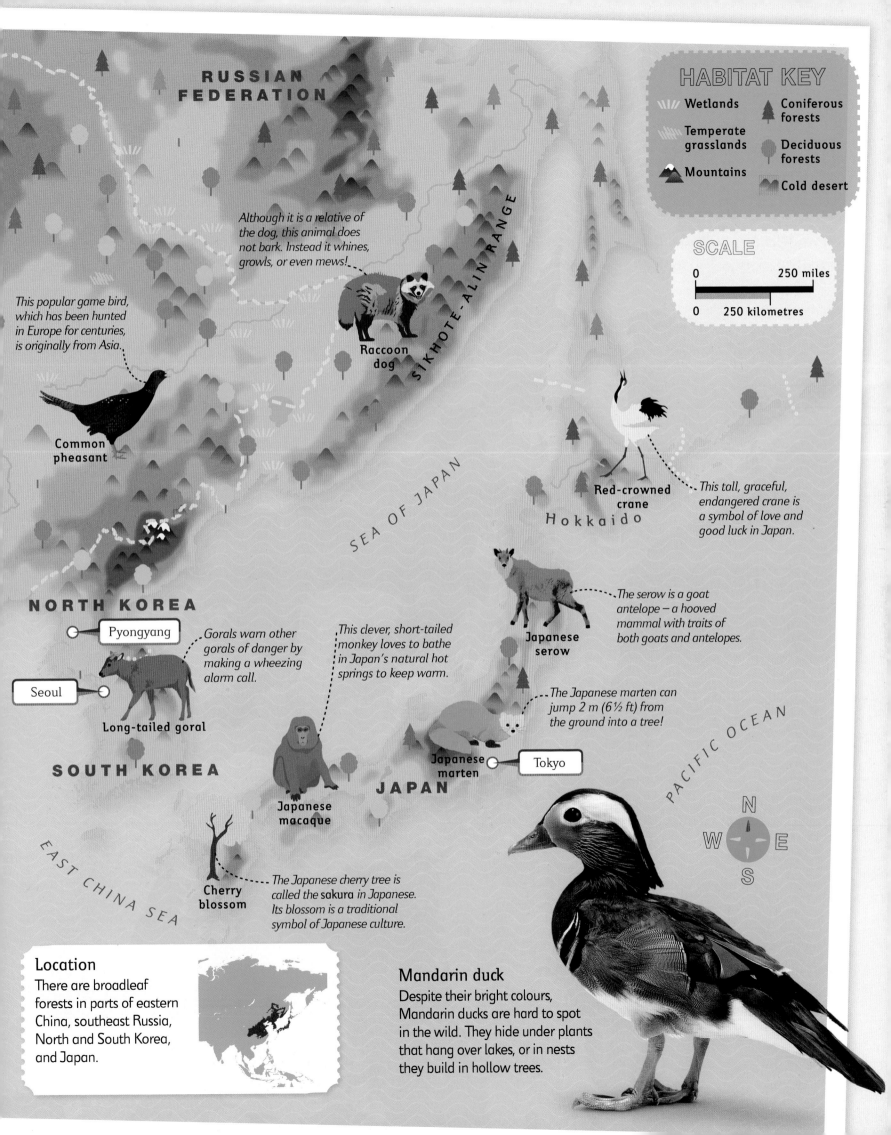

RUSSIAN FEDERATION

Wetlands

Temperate grasslands

Mountains

Coniferous forests

Deciduous forests

Cold desert

SCALE

0 ——— 250 miles

0 ——— 250 kilometres

Although it is a relative of the dog, this animal does not bark. Instead it whines, growls, or even mews!

Raccoon dog

SIKHOTE-ALIN RANGE

This popular game bird, which has been hunted in Europe for centuries, is originally from Asia.

Common pheasant

Red-crowned crane

Hokkaido

This tall, graceful, endangered crane is a symbol of love and good luck in Japan.

SEA OF JAPAN

NORTH KOREA

Pyongyang

Gorals warn other gorals of danger by making a wheezing alarm call.

Seoul

Long-tailed goral

This clever, short-tailed monkey loves to bathe in Japan's natural hot springs to keep warm.

Japanese serow

The serow is a goat antelope – a hooved mammal with traits of both goats and antelopes.

The Japanese marten can jump 2 m (6½ ft) from the ground into a tree!

SOUTH KOREA

JAPAN

Japanese marten

Tokyo

Japanese macaque

PACIFIC OCEAN

EAST CHINA SEA

Cherry blossom

The Japanese cherry tree is called the sakura in Japanese. Its blossom is a traditional symbol of Japanese culture.

N W E S

Location

There are broadleaf forests in parts of eastern China, southeast Russia, North and South Korea, and Japan.

Mandarin duck

Despite their bright colours, Mandarin ducks are hard to spot in the wild. They hide under plants that hang over lakes, or in nests they build in hollow trees.

Arabian Peninsula

The Arabian Peninsula is a hot, dry part of the world, and it is covered by sandy deserts. The animals that live here have special ways of coping with its harsh conditions.

Arabian partridge
This partridge lives on the ground, where it looks for seeds, grass, and insects to eat. The female lays her eggs in a shallow, scooped-out hole.

Partridges run rather than fly away when threatened.

Location
Located between Africa and Asia, the Arabian Peninsula is made up of Saudi Arabia and several smaller countries.

JORDAN

ISRAEL

IRAQ

IRAN

BAHRAIN

QATAR

UNITED ARAB EMIRATES

SAUDI ARABIA

OMAN

YEMEN

RED SEA

N E S W

This cat can jump 3 m (10 ft) off the ground to snatch birds out of the air.

Caracal

Spade-like hooves let this antelope walk on the soft desert sand with ease.

Arabian oryx

People of the desert, called the Bedouin, bred this horse to be fast, strong, and able to withstand desert conditions.

Arabian horse

Riyadh

Fur on the bottom of its feet help the sand cat walk over hot ground.

Sand cat

The sand fish is a type of lizard that "swims" beneath the surface of the sand using its flipper-like feet.

Sand fish

Muscat

Mountain gazelle

Male gazelles have "air-cushion" fights — they charge at each other but stop just before they crash.

SCALE
0 — 200 miles
0 — 200 kilometres

The camel spider isn't a true spider — it's a different type of arachnid, and it eats scorpions, spiders, and mice.

Arabian camel spider

Sana'a

Hamadryas baboon
These monkeys live in troops of up to 1,000. They spend nights on ledges of cliffs, but come down to the ground each day to find food.

HABITAT KEY
Wetlands
Mountains
Deciduous forests
Hot desert

Rock hyrax
Although it looks more like a guinea pig, the plant-eating rock hyrax is related to the elephant. It even grows two tiny tusks!

India's forests can be wet or dry, but all are warm and tropical. Many trees have broad leaves that they lose in the dry season. For animals, the forests provide food and shelter. However, as trees are cut down for wood, or to make farmland, animals like the Bengal tiger have fewer places to live.

Location

Indian forests stretch from the Himalayan mountains south to the Indian Ocean. The weather here is hot or warm most of the year.

PAKISTAN

Ganges

Yamuna

INDIA

New Delhi

Male peafowl are called peacocks. They use their bright, eye-spotted feathers to attract mates.

Ganges

Bengal tiger
This tiger's canine teeth (fangs) grow up to 10 cm (4 in) long.

Peafowl

Narmada

Indian grey mongoose
Mongooses kill scorpions by throwing them against a hard surface until they crack.

The cobra hunts lizards, rodents, and frogs. Venom from its bite stops its prey from being able to move.

Godavani

Indian cobra

The Indian rhino's horn grows to 60 cm (2 ft) long. It's made from keratin – just like our hair.

Krishna

Indian rhinoceros

N
W E
S

The Indian giant hornet's bright orange colour makes it easy to spot.

Indian giant hornet

The giant hornet is the world's largest – and probably angriest – wasp. It grows up to 5 cm (2 in) long and will sting anything that even slightly disturbs its nest.

The giant squirrel builds nests in trees that are the same size as eagles' nests.

Indian giant squirrel

ARABIAN SEA

BAY OF BENGAL

Andaman and Nicobar islands

Asia's largest land mammal is much smaller than its African cousin. It spends three-quarters of its day eating plants.

SCALE

0 — 200 miles

0 — 200 kilometres

Asian elephant

SRI LANKA

Colombo

Sri Jayawardenepura Kotte

Sloth bear

The shy sloth bear digs ants and termites with its long, curved claws. As it laps them up, its loud slurping can be heard from several kilometres away.

HABITAT KEY

- Wetlands
- Mountains
- Cold desert
- Coniferous forests
- Deciduous forests
- Tropical forests

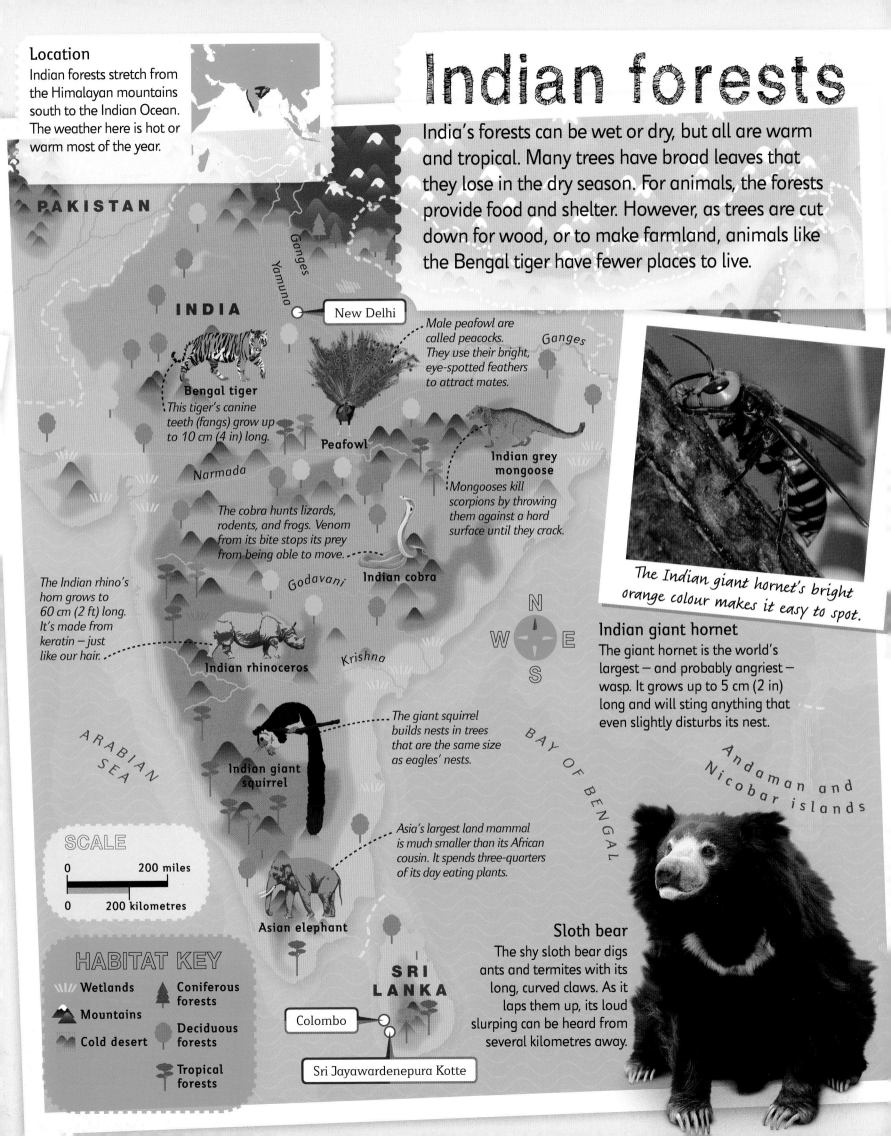

Female orchid mantises look like flowers. Males are smaller and duller in colour.

Orchid mantis

This insect disguises itself as a pink-and-white orchid flower. When other insects land nearby, they are caught unaware as the mantis strikes.

Bornean orangutan

Fruit-eating orangutans live in trees. They bend branches into nests to sleep in at night. Orangutans live on their own, unlike other great apes.

Southeast Asian rainforest

The Southeast Asian rainforests are some of the oldest on Earth, and they are home to hundreds of animal species. As the rainforests are cut down, however, amazing animals like the Sumatran rhinoceros become rarer and rarer.

INDIA

CHINA

MYANMAR

VIETNAM

Nay Pyi Daw

Hanoi

LAOS

Vientiane

Hainan

Adult sunbirds drink nectar with their long, curved bills. They feed their chicks insects.

Lar gibbon

Purple sunbird

Gibbons sing in the treetops every morning to tell other gibbons where their territory is.

Bangkok

CAMBODIA

ANDAMAN SEA

Its fox-like face gives this large fruit bat its name.

Water buffalo

Andaman Islands

Large flying fox

Phnom Penh

The domesticated water buffalo is widely used to plough paddy (rice) fields.

THAILAND

GULF OF THAILAND

This frog jumps from tree to tree, using its webbed feet and loose skin like a parachute.

Wallace's flying frog

Special skin stretched over extra-long ribs lets this lizard glide through the rainforest.

Nicobar Islands

This rare, endangered rainforest rhino has two horns.

Sumatran rhinoceros

MALAYSIA

Putrajaya

Kuala Lumpur

Common flying dragon

SINGAPORE

Sumatra

Borneo

This is the biggest single flower in the world. It smells like rotting flesh!

Rafflesia flower

Jakarta

INDIAN OCEAN

Java

Taipei

TAIWAN

Location

Lots of countries make up Southeast Asia, including many island nations. All are tropical, with a rainy monsoon season and a hot, dry season.

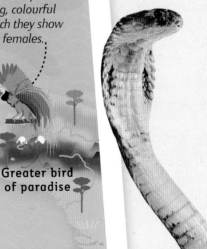

One sting from a ribbontail stingray can kill a would-be predator.

HABITAT KEY

- Wetlands
- Tropical forests
- Mountains

SCALE

0 ——— 200 miles

0 ——— 200 kilometres

A big "sail" of skin on its tail helps drive the soa-soa water lizard forwards when it swims.

Soa-soa water lizard

Manila

SOUTH CHINA SEA

Ribbontail stingray

This stingray swims in shallow water, looking for crabs, shrimp, and small fish to eat. Its bright-blue spots and stripes warn other sea creatures to stay away.

PHILIPPINES

PACIFIC OCEAN

SULU SEA

Just 16 cm (6 in) tall, this little primate can turn its head right around to look backwards!

Philippine tarsier

Palau

This species of humpback dolphin is usually grey, but it can also be white, or even pink!

King cobra

The king cobra can grow up to 5.5 m (18 ft) long. It lives almost entirely off other snakes, which it hunts by sight and smell. Unusually, this snake doesn't hiss — it growls!

BRUNEI

The world's smallest type of bear uses its long tongue to lap up insects, but its favourite food is fruit.

Sun bear

Indo-Pacific humpback dolphin

MOLUCCA SEA

North Maluku

Only male birds of paradise have amazing, colourful feathers, which they show off to attract females.

New Guinea

INDONESIA

Proboscis monkey

Sulawesi

Maluku

Greater bird of paradise

Male proboscis monkeys' massive noses help to make their calls louder.

The world's biggest lizard, the komodo dragon grows up to 2 m (6 ft) long. Its venomous bite can kill a water buffalo!

JAVA SEA

EAST TIMOR

Bali

Komodo dragon

Dili

Gobi Desert

The Gobi is Asia's largest desert. It spans more than 1.2 million sq km (460,000 sq miles). Temperatures here can be as scorching hot as 50°C (122°F) and as freezing cold as -40°C (-40°F), but many tough animal species are able to survive despite the extreme conditions.

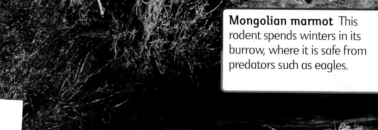

Gobi bear This is the Earth's rarest bear. Fewer than 50 Gobi bears remain in the desert, their only home.

Mongolian wild ass The wild ass waits for rare rain showers. After the showers, it can feed on fresh grass.

Dinosaur fossil
The Gobi tells us a lot about prehistoric wildlife. Hundreds of dinosaur fossils of many types have been found here — including some from 250 million years ago! This was also first place in the world where dinosaur eggs were identified.

Mongolian marmot This rodent spends winters in its burrow, where it is safe from predators such as eagles.

Long-eared jerboa This tiny, mouse-like jerboa hops about the desert at night, looking for tasty insects to eat.

This jerboa's enormous ears are almost as long as its body! Scientists think they release heat, keeping the jerboa cool.

Marbled polecat
This little predator doesn't see very well, but it has no trouble finding most of its prey by smell. It hunts rodents, birds, and reptiles — mainly during cool desert nights.

Marbled polecats are named after the pattern on their backs.

Great bustard Each year, male great bustards grow "whiskers" that look a lot like ears of wheat!

The great bustard flies with slow, steady beats of its wings, which end in long, white feathers.

Yarkand gazelle Unlike other gazelles, the Yarkland doesn't "bound". If scared, it sprints away as fast as it can!

Bactrian camel

The Bactrian camel has two humps, where it stores fat to help it survive for long periods without food. If it can't find enough plants to eat, it will eat bones, rope, or even a tent!

Przewalski's wild horse This wild horse is always on the move, looking for water and short grasses to eat.

Saxaul tree

The gnarly saxaul has a lot of roots to anchor it in the sand. Its tiny leaves keep it from losing too much moisture, and it stores water in its bark. If you press a few pieces together, water comes out!

Location

The Gobi stretches across northwestern China and southern Mongolia. The average rainfall here is just 190 mm (less than 8 in) a year.

Australasia

Australia, New Zealand, Papua New Guinea, and thousands of small islands make up the Australasia region. From deserts, mountains, and rainforests to beaches and coral reefs, the habitats here are home to many animals only found in this part of the world.

PHILIPPINE SEA

Northern Mariana Islands **(UNITED STATES)**

Guam **(UNITED STATES)**

MICRONESIA

PALAU

Australian coast
The western Australian coast is home to hundreds of fish, mammals, and bird species. Australian pelicans often land here to enjoy the sand and sun after staying in the air for 24 hours!

PAPUA NEW GUINEA

ARAFURA SEA

TIMOR SEA

Christmas Island **(AUSTRALIA)**

Ashmore and Cartier Islands **(AUSTRALIA)**

Coral Sea Islands **(AUSTRALIA)**

CORAL SEA

Cocos (Keeling) Islands **(AUSTRALIA)**

Northern Territory

Queensland

INDIAN OCEAN

AUSTRALIA

Western Australia

South Australia

New South Wales

N
W   E
S

Victoria

Australian Outback
The hot, dry centre of Australia is known as the Outback, or the "bush". As it is mainly desert, very few people live here, but some amazing animals have found ways to survive the tough desert conditions.

Tasmania

Snares Islands
This New Zealand island group, north of the Auckland Islands, is protected from humans so native animal species can thrive. One is the Snares penguin, which nests only on these islands — on the ground, under trees and shrubs.

Macquarie Island **(AUSTRALIA)**

New Guinea forests

Forests cover two-thirds of the island of Papua New Guinea. Around 760 bird species and 25,000 plant species live here, as does the Goodfellow's tree kangaroo, which climbs trees to eat leaves.

Coral reefs

Coral reefs, like this one in French Polynesia, make up about one per cent of the ocean floor — but they are home to almost a quarter of all ocean species. Lots of fish, such as these gold-lined sea breams, gather in the reefs to eat.

Wake Island
(UNITED STATES)

MARSHALL ISLANDS

NAURU

Kingman Reef
(UNITED STATES)

Baker and Howland Islands
(UNITED STATES)

Palmyra Atoll
(UNITED STATES)

Jarvis Island
(UNITED STATES)

K I R I B A T I

SOLOMON ISLANDS

TUVALU

Wallis and Futuna
(FRANCE)

SAMOA

V A N U A T U

American Samoa
(UNITED STATES)

FIJI

New Caledonia
(FRANCE)

Niue
(NEW ZEALAND)

TONGA

Cook Islands
(NEW ZEALAND)

Norfolk Island
(AUSTRALIA)

Kermadec Islands
(NEW ZEALAND)

French Polynesia
(FRANCE)

Lord Howe Island
(AUSTRALIA)

PACIFIC OCEAN

NEW ZEALAND

TASMAN SEA

Pitcairn, Henderson, Ducie, and Oeno Islands
(UNITED KINGDOM)

Chatham Islands
(NEW ZEALAND)

Bounty Islands
(NEW ZEALAND)

Antipodes Islands
(NEW ZEALAND)

Auckland Islands
(NEW ZEALAND)

Campbell Islands
(NEW ZEALAND)

HABITAT KEY

- Tropical forests
- Deciduous forests
- Tropical grasslands
- Scrublands
- Temperate grasslands
- Desert
- Mountains
- Mangroves

SCALE

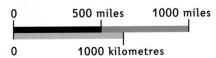

0   500 miles   1000 miles

0   1000 kilometres

Australia

Australia is the world's largest island. Most of it is made of hot, dry desert called "the Outback". In the hottest months, some of Australia's lakes may dry up completely. However, there are rainforests here, too, and many of the animals that live in Australia are found nowhere else.

This lizard defends itself by opening its frill, standing on its hind legs, and hissing.

Frilled lizard

The kookaburra is the largest kingfisher. Its call sounds like a laugh.

Blue-winged kookaburra

Victoria

Fitzroy

INDIAN OCEAN

Location

Australia lies south of the Equator, between the Pacific and Indian oceans. Summer here is from December to February.

This desert lizard is covered in protective thorny scales.

De Grey

Fortescue

Thorny devil

Ashburton

AUSTRALIA

HABITAT KEY

Temperate grasslands	Tropical forests
Scrublands	Mountains
Tropical grasslands	Hot desert

Gascoyne

These huge caterpillars eat witchetty bush roots — and Australian Aboriginals, the first people to live here, eat them!

Witchetty grubs

Common off the Australian coast, the world's largest predatory fish has 300 teeth.

This mouse-sized marsupial doesn't eat honey — just nectar and pollen.

Honey possum

Great white shark

Emu
Australia's largest bird is 1.5–2 m (5–6½ ft) tall and can weigh up to 60 kg (132 lb). Its call can be heard up to 2 km (1 mile) away!

N
W   E
S

Red kangaroo
Kangaroos are marsupials. A marsupial is a type of animal that carries its young in a pouch on its body. Red kangaroos are only found in Australia. They move by hopping around on their powerful back legs.

A baby kangaroo, called a joey, rides in its mother's pouch.

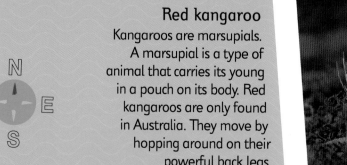

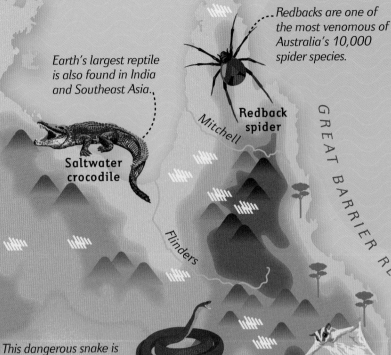

PAPUA NEW GUINEA

Earth's largest reptile is also found in India and Southeast Asia.

Saltwater crocodile

Redbacks are one of the most venomous of Australia's 10,000 spider species.

Redback spider

Mitchell

Flinders

GREAT BARRIER REEF

This dangerous snake is responsible for the most deaths by snakebite in Australia. Watch out!

Eastern brown snake

Sugar glider

A webbed membrane allows this tiny mammal to glide more than 46 m (151 ft) between trees.

This intelligent wild dog rarely barks, but it loves to howl.

Dingo

This plant-eating burrower is a marsupial, but its pouch points backwards. Also, its poo is cubed-shaped!

Common wombat

BLUE MOUNTAINS

Darling

Platypus

Murray

Canberra

This egg-laying mammal has webbed feet and a duck-like bill.

TASMAN SEA

GREAT AUSTRALIAN BIGHT

This animal is the size of a small dog. It's called a devil as it is so aggressive.

Tasmanian devil

The short-beaked echidna's sharp spines repel predators.

Short-beaked echidna
Also called the spiny anteater, this strange-looking mammal lays eggs. It uses its long, sticky tongue to eat grubs, termites, and ants.

Koala
Often mistakenly called bears, koalas are marsupials. Once big enough to leave the pouch, baby koalas ride on the parents' backs. Koalas mainly eat eucalyptus (gum tree) leaves, such as those found in southeastern Australia.

79

New Zealand

New Zealand is made up of two main islands — North and South Island — and many smaller ones. Lots of birds live here, some of which cannot fly. Unfortunately, many were killed by cats, rats, and other predators brought by European settlers. Now, rare birds such as the kakapo are protected.

Auckland tree weta

Wetas are much larger cousins of crickets. A tree weta's body is around 4 cm (1½ in) long, but a giant weta can be 10 cm (4 in) — longer than your hand!

Auckland tree wetas can raise their spiny back legs for defence.

Kauri

These massive trees grow only on the North Island. Birds eat the seeds from the cones they produce.

Southern right whale

This bus-sized whale often raises its tail like a sail, letting the wind push it along the surface of the ocean.

New Zealand lesser short-tailed bat

Bats are New Zealand's only native mammals. This one spends more time on the ground than in the air.

New Zealand land snail

This massive snail grows to 9 cm (3½ in) across and loves to eat earthworms.

North Island brown kiwi

New Zealand's national symbol, the kiwi is a bird that cannot fly. It lives mainly in burrows and only comes out at night.

Hamilton's frog

This rare frog lives mainly on tiny Stephens Island, where it is safe from tuataras and rats.

BAY OF PLENTY

North Island

Hawke Bay

Lake Taupo

Waikato

Wellington

TASMAN SEA

N E S W

SCALE

0   250 miles

0   250 kilometres

Location

Located in the southwestern Pacific Ocean, New Zealand's nearest neighbour is Australia, 1,500 km (932 miles) to the northwest.

Its large eyes help the nocturnal morepork to see at night.

Morepork
This small, dark owl got its name because its call sounds like "more pork"! It sleeps in forests during the day. At night it hunts insects, such as the weta.

Kea
Scientists think this cat-sized parrot is as clever as a four-year-old child. It lives on the South Island and makes a laugh-like squeal.

PACIFIC OCEAN

Tuatara
This reptile's closest relatives were around at the time of the dinosaurs. Tuataras like cool weather and can live for up to 100 years!

Also called the kereru, this blue-green bird eats mostly fruit. It has a red bill, eyes, and feet.

New Zealand pigeon

The yellow-eyed penguin lays its eggs in forests, and hunts for food up to 24 km (15 miles) away.

Yellow-eyed penguin

This sea lion rests on southern beaches and offshore islands when it isn't hunting squid.

New Zealand sea lion

Found only in New Zealand, this crayfish buries itself in mud to survive droughts.

Northern koura

South Island

Lake Tekapo
Lake Pukaki
Lake Ohau

Clutha

So rare they are almost extinct, these large, flightless parrots live only in New Zealand.

Kakapo

Stewart Island

Highly endangered, this sociable little dolphin only grows up to 1.4 m (4½ ft) long.

Hector's dolphin

SOUTHERN ALPS

Lake Hawea
Lake Wanaka

Blue damselfly

Lake Te Anau

TASMAN SEA

The blue damselfly can turn itself darker to get more warmth from the Sun.

81

Great Barrier Reef

The world's largest chain of coral reefs, the Great Barrier Reef lies just off Australia's northeastern coast. It's so big that it can be seen from space, and it is home to more than 1,500 types of fish.

Regal tang Also called surgeonfish, tangs have a scalpel-like spine at the base of their tail on both sides.

Dugongs can live for 70 years or more in the wild.

Giant barrel sponge The barrel sponge is an animal that grows up to 1.8 m (6 ft) across – and it has no brain!

Sea slug Sea slugs eat corals, sea anemones, sponges, and fish eggs. Their bright colours warn predators away.

Dugong

This slow-moving mammal eats nothing but plants. It pulls seagrass out by the roots with its flexible upper lip. Dugongs are also called "sea cows", because they graze like cows.

Coral

Living corals are made up of tiny animals called coral polyps that catch bits of food with their tentacles. The polyps make hard cases from minerals to protect themselves, and these build up over many years into reef.

Blue starfish Tiny suckers, called tube feet, cover the underside of starfish and let them crawl over the reef.

The reef has many different types of coral. As well as hard corals, which build the reef, there are also soft corals.

Starfish can regrow a damaged or lost arm. Some can even grow a whole new starfish from just part of an arm.

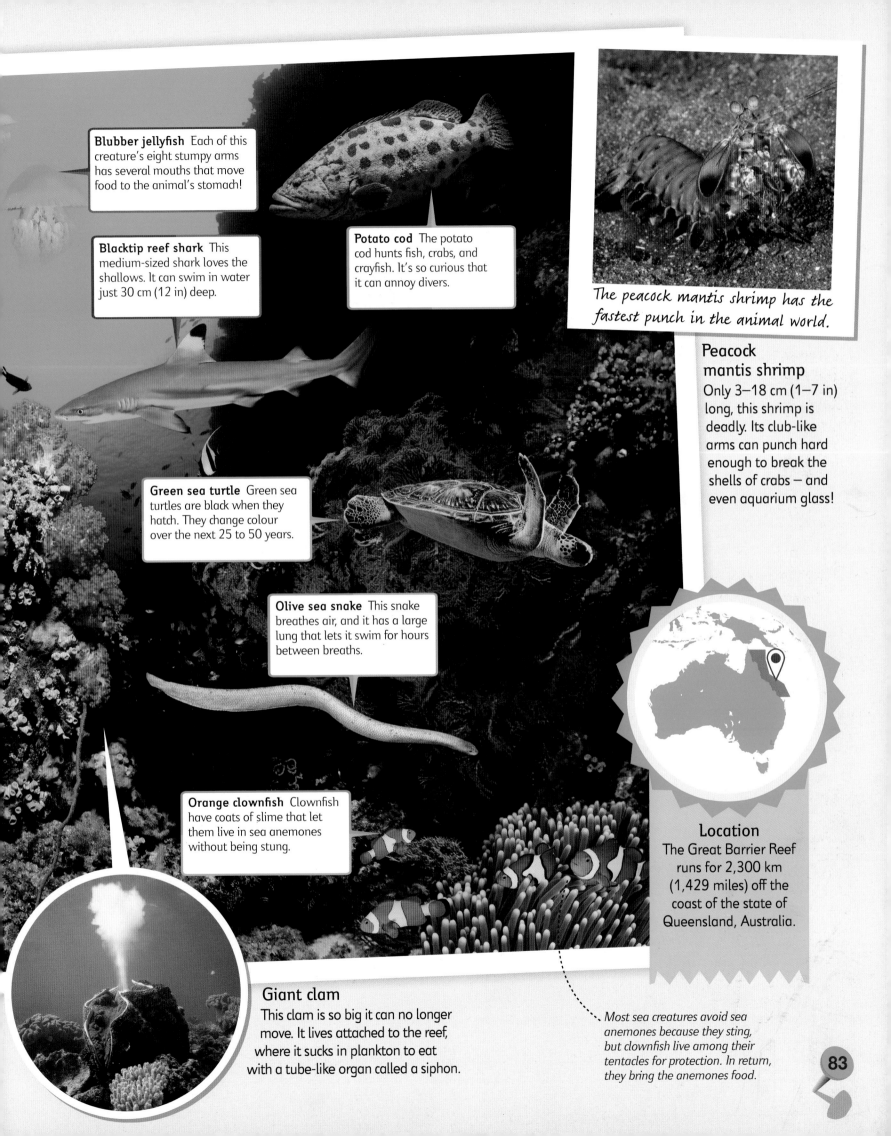

Blubber jellyfish Each of this creature's eight stumpy arms has several mouths that move food to the animal's stomach!

Blacktip reef shark This medium-sized shark loves the shallows. It can swim in water just 30 cm (12 in) deep.

Potato cod The potato cod hunts fish, crabs, and crayfish. It's so curious that it can annoy divers.

The peacock mantis shrimp has the fastest punch in the animal world.

Peacock mantis shrimp
Only 3–18 cm (1–7 in) long, this shrimp is deadly. Its club-like arms can punch hard enough to break the shells of crabs — and even aquarium glass!

Green sea turtle Green sea turtles are black when they hatch. They change colour over the next 25 to 50 years.

Olive sea snake This snake breathes air, and it has a large lung that lets it swim for hours between breaths.

Location
The Great Barrier Reef runs for 2,300 km (1,429 miles) off the coast of the state of Queensland, Australia.

Orange clownfish Clownfish have coats of slime that let them live in sea anemones without being stung.

Giant clam
This clam is so big it can no longer move. It lives attached to the reef, where it sucks in plankton to eat with a tube-like organ called a siphon.

Most sea creatures avoid sea anemones because they sting, but clownfish live among their tentacles for protection. In return, they bring the anemones food.

Antarctica

The world's coldest continent, Antarctica is also its most remote, meaning it is far from any other land mass. Ice more than 1.6 km (1 mile) thick covers most of it, and temperatures go down to -89.2°C (-129°F), too extreme for many animals. As it doesn't rain here, Antarctica is considered a desert.

Location
Antarctica is found at the bottom of the Earth. It is home to the Earth's most southerly point, the South Pole.

HABITAT KEY

 Snow and ice   🏔 Mountains

Southern elephant seal
The southern elephant seal is Earth's largest seal. Males can grow up to 6 m (19⅔ ft) long and weigh 3,856 kg (8,501 lb), but females are much smaller. An inflatable, trunk-like nose allows males to make loud roaring calls.

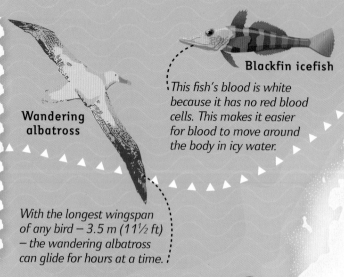

Wandering albatross

Blackfin icefish

This fish's blood is white because it has no red blood cells. This makes it easier for blood to move around the body in icy water.

With the longest wingspan of any bird – 3.5 m (11½ ft) – the wandering albatross can glide for hours at a time.

Weddell seals can stay underwater for up to 82 minutes while they hunt for icefish.

Weddell seal

ANTARCTIC PENINSULA

WEDDELL SEA

FILCHNER ICE SHELF

RONNE ICE SHELF

Chinstrap penguin

These penguins look as if they have a strap around their chin. They are often found on icebergs in the sea around Antarctica.

Unlike most Antarctic fish, the toothfish has chemicals in its blood that prevent it from freezing.

Patagonian toothfish

TO SOUTH AMERICA

West Antarctica

This small whale eats krill by using comb-like structures in its mouth called baleen.

Antarctic minke whale

Limit of winter pack ice

TO NEW ZEALAND

Limit of summer pack ice

SOUTHERN OCEAN

SCALE
0 ———— 250 miles

0 ———— 250 kilometres

Even though it has enormous jaws and eats other animals, this seal's main food is tiny krill.

Leopard seal

Krill are tiny, shrimp-like crustaceans that provide food for animals ranging from small fish to the largest whales.

Antarctic krill

Antarctic brittle star

This relative of the starfish can lose an arm if attacked – and grow it back again!

TO AFRICA

Pure white apart from their black eyes and bills, snow petrels have even been seen at the South Pole.

Snow petrel

The colossal squid is the biggest squid on Earth. It also has the largest eyes of any animal.

Colossal squid

E a s t
A n t a r c t i c a

The size of a large gull, the skua takes penguin eggs and chicks for food.

South polar skua

T R A N S A N T A R C T I C
M O U N T A I N S

This penguin is 71 cm (28 in) high and makes its nest out of stones, sometimes stealing rocks from its neighbours.

Adélie penguin

TO AUSTRALIA

The Antarctic midge looks tiny when shown on a human finger.

Antarctic midge

Antarctica's only insect, this midge lives on the rocky Antarctic Peninsula, which juts out into the Southern Ocean. It is wingless and eats algae and bacteria. Adult midges live just seven to ten days, but their young can survive two winters.

Emperor penguin

The emperor penguin is the only animal to survive Antarctica's ice in winter. It stays snug with its waterproof coat and four layers of feathers. Males keep the eggs warm by holding them on their feet off of the chilly ice.

Emperor penguin chicks are covered in fluffy grey down, which is not waterproof.

The Arctic

The Arctic is the Earth's northernmost region. Animals here must survive freezing temperatures. Ice and snow cover the area in winter, and the water of the Arctic Ocean freezes over. In summer, much of the ice melts, revealing a treeless habitat on the surrounding land called tundra.

Polar bear

The polar bear actually has black skin, but it is covered by thick fur to keep the bear warm. A strong swimmer, the polar bear hunts seals, which it can smell from 1.6 km (1 mile) away.

A polar bear's white fur helps it to blend in with its habitat.

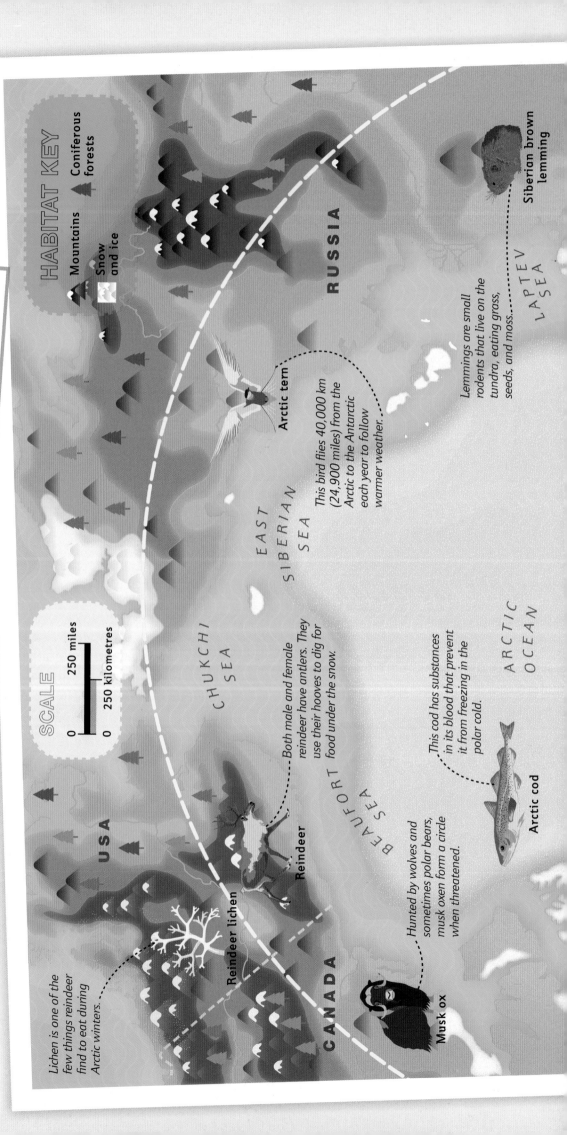

HABITAT KEY

▲ Mountains   ▲ Coniferous forests

◳ Snow and ice

RUSSIA

Lemmings are small rodents that live on the tundra, eating grass, seeds, and moss.

Siberian brown lemming

LAPTEV SEA

Arctic tern

This bird flies 40,000 km (24,900 miles) from the Arctic to the Antarctic each year to follow warmer weather.

EAST SIBERIAN SEA

CHUKCHI SEA

SCALE

0 ___ 250 miles

0 ___ 250 kilometres

Both male and female reindeer have antlers. They use their hooves to dig for food under the snow.

Reindeer

This cod has substances in its blood that prevent it from freezing in the polar cold.

Arctic cod

BEAUFORT SEA

ARCTIC OCEAN

USA

Reindeer lichen

Lichen is one of the few things reindeer find to eat during Arctic winters.

Hunted by wolves and sometimes polar bears, musk oxen form a circle when threatened.

CANADA

Musk ox

ARCTIC CIRCLE

Snowy owl

Lemmings are one of the snowy owl's main sources of food. It can eat five lemmings in a day.

An adult harp seal watches its white-furred cub.

KARA SEA

BARENTS SEA

Born grey, beluga whales don't turn white until they are as old as eight years.

Beluga

Greenland shark

A very slow swimmer, this shark cruises deep in the ocean, feeding on carrion (dead animals).

Narwhal

This whale's spiral tusk is actually a tooth that grows up to 3 m (10 ft) long.

● North Pole

Walrus

A thick layer of blubber (fat) keeps walruses warm when they hunt for food in icy waters.

GREENLAND SEA

NORWAY

FINLAND

SWEDEN

Harp seal

These seals are named for the pattern on their backs, which looks like the musical instrument. Harp seals are born white, but turn dark after three weeks.

Location
The Arctic includes the extreme northern parts of Europe, Asia, and North America. Winters get as cold as -68°C (-90°F).

Arctic fox

In summer, the Arctic fox sheds its white coat, turning grey-brown so it blends in with its surroundings.

Arctic hare

Its pure-white coat makes this hare almost invisible in the snow.

Arctic fox

In winter, this fox turns white to help it to hide in the snow as it hunts for Arctic hares.

GREENLAND (DENMARK)

HABITAT KEY
 Coral reef

The chinook hatches in fresh water, then swims to the sea, but each adult fish returns to the place where it hatched to breed.

Chinook salmon

Common cuttlefish

The cuttlefish changes colour to blend in with its surroundings and to communicate with other cuttlefish. It has three hearts, two of which pump blood to its gills. The third pumps blood around its body.

The cuttlefish is related to squids and octopuses.

As it grows, the lobster sheds its skin – a process called moulting. By the time it becomes an adult, a lobster has increased in size 100,000 times!

Sardines grow up to 30 cm (12 in) long and swim in massive schools with lots of other sardines so they aren't all eaten at once!

Sardines

Killer whale

Also known as an orca, this is the largest dolphin species. It has teeth up to 10 cm (4 in) long.

American lobster

Blue mussels

The blue mussel is one of the toughest shellfish around. It can survive freezing as well as very warm ocean water.

The world's largest ray, the giant manta grows up to 7 m (23 ft) across and weighs up to 2 tonnes (2.2 tons).

Giant manta ray

Yellowfin tuna

Just one yellowfin tuna can weigh up to 400 kg (882 lb), although 176 kg (388 lb) is more common.

The great hammerhead's favourite food is the stingray. It holds rays down using one side of its "hammer" to avoid getting stung while it feeds!

Great hammerhead

The seahorse can move its eyes individually, so it can watch for predators or prey from many directions at once.

Spiny seahorse

PACIFIC OCEAN

The footballfish uses the glowing lure on its head to tempt passing prey close enough to eat.

Deep sea footballfish

ATLANTIC OCEAN

Oceans and seas

Water covers a huge 70 per cent of the Earth's surface. Thousands of species live in or near oceans and seas, from tiny plankton to the largest creature on our planet — the blue whale.

The blue whale is roughly the size of a jumbo jet. It weighs two times more than the biggest known dinosaur.

Blue whale

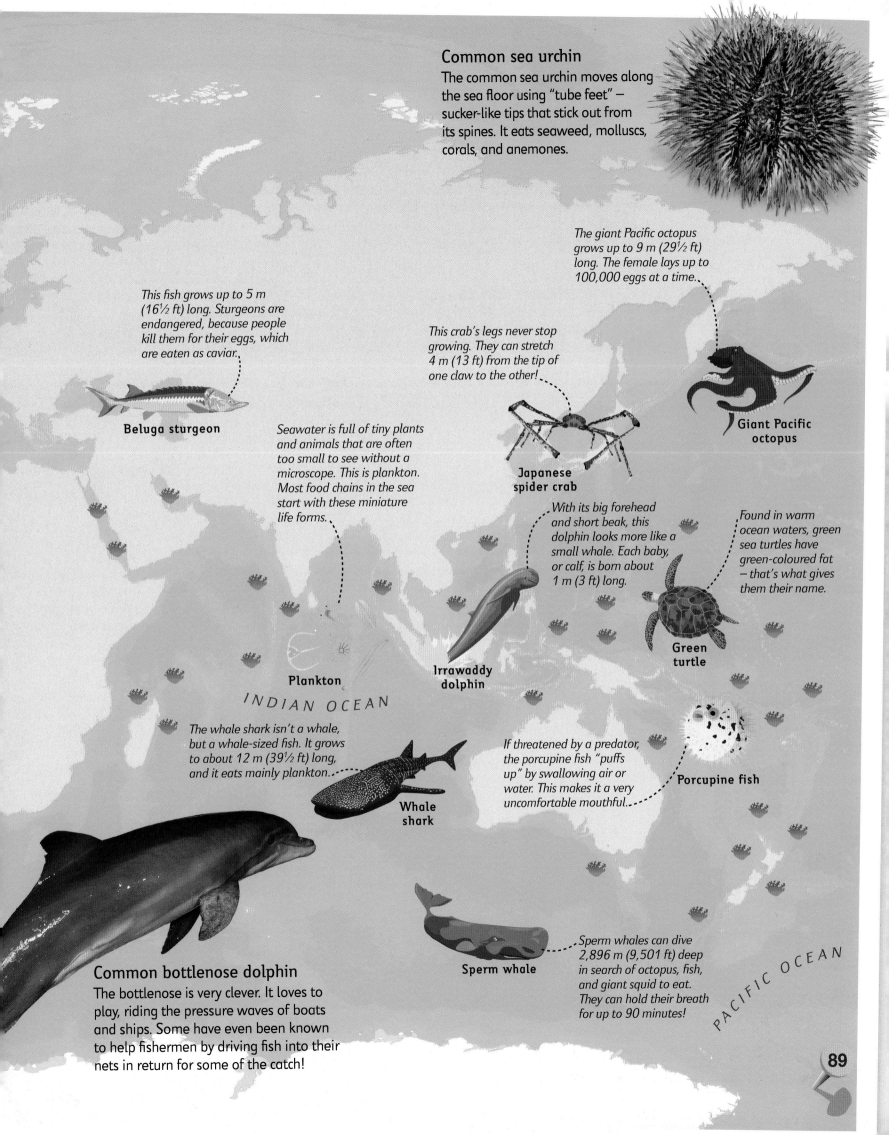

Common sea urchin

The common sea urchin moves along the sea floor using "tube feet" — sucker-like tips that stick out from its spines. It eats seaweed, molluscs, corals, and anemones.

The giant Pacific octopus grows up to 9 m (29½ ft) long. The female lays up to 100,000 eggs at a time.

This fish grows up to 5 m (16½ ft) long. Sturgeons are endangered, because people kill them for their eggs, which are eaten as caviar.

This crab's legs never stop growing. They can stretch 4 m (13 ft) from the tip of one claw to the other!

Giant Pacific octopus

Beluga sturgeon

Seawater is full of tiny plants and animals that are often too small to see without a microscope. This is plankton. Most food chains in the sea start with these miniature life forms.

Japanese spider crab

With its big forehead and short beak, this dolphin looks more like a small whale. Each baby, or calf, is born about 1 m (3 ft) long.

Found in warm ocean waters, green sea turtles have green-coloured fat — that's what gives them their name.

Plankton

INDIAN OCEAN

Irrawaddy dolphin

Green turtle

The whale shark isn't a whale, but a whale-sized fish. It grows to about 12 m (39½ ft) long, and it eats mainly plankton.

If threatened by a predator, the porcupine fish "puffs up" by swallowing air or water. This makes it a very uncomfortable mouthful.

Porcupine fish

Whale shark

Common bottlenose dolphin

The bottlenose is very clever. It loves to play, riding the pressure waves of boats and ships. Some have even been known to help fishermen by driving fish into their nets in return for some of the catch!

Sperm whale

Sperm whales can dive 2,896 m (9,501 ft) deep in search of octopus, fish, and giant squid to eat. They can hold their breath for up to 90 minutes!

PACIFIC OCEAN

ATLAS PICTURE QUIZ

This area in northern Africa is the largest hot desert in the world.

1

2

This area of scrubland shares its name with the sea it borders.

This high prairie stretches across parts of Canada and the United States.

3

10

This famous mountain range in Europe includes lakes, glaciers, meadows, and forests.

NAME THE HABITAT

Here are some of the habitats and islands that appear in this atlas. Can you name them? Look at the clues to help you. The answers are on page 91.

4

This country is made of two main islands and lots of other, smaller ones.

9

This desert in southern Africa gets enough rain for grass and other plants to grow.

This South American rainforest is home to 2.5 million different species of insects.

5

The rainforests of this area are some of the oldest on Earth.

8

7

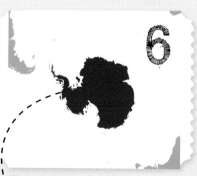

6

These volcanic islands are home to many unique animals named after the area.

This continent, found at the bottom of the Earth, is the world's coldest.

All of the answers to these questions appear somewhere in this book. You can check if you are correct at the bottom of this page.

3. How many ants can an aardvark eat a night?

2. Which sea creature has the largest eyes of any animal?

1. Which is the smallest of the "big cats"?

4. What colour, other than blue, can the Mediterranean tree frog be?

5. For how long does a seven-spot ladybird live?

6. In which mountain range would you find the spectacled bear?

7. How long do the Iberian ibex's horns grow?

11. In which area would you find a mandrill?

10. Which is the largest tortoise in Africa?

9. Where does the Gila monster live?

8. Which animal has cube-shaped poo?

12. Which lizard is also called the racerunner?

13. Which bird has two tail feathers twice the length of its body?

14. Which whale has a tusk that can grow to 3 m (10 ft) long?

15. On which island does the ring-tailed lemur live?

19. Which butterfly migrates from northern North America to Mexico?

18. Which penguin lays its eggs in forests?

17. What is the heaviest spider in the world?

16. What is the heaviest flying bird on Earth?

20. Which bat drinks other animals' blood?

21. How long can the Indian tiger's fangs grow?

22. Which frog uses its feet to parachute from tree to tree?

23. Which beetle with antler-like jaws is this?

Answers: **Page 90 Name the habitat:** 1. Sahara desert (pages 36–37), 2. Kalahari (page 12), 3. Great Plains (page 42), 4. New Zealand (pages 80–81), 5. Amazon rainforest (pages 22–23), 6. Antarctica (pages 84–85), 7. Southeast Asia (pages 72–73), 8. The Galápagos (page 29), 9. Mediterranean scrubland (pages 56–57), 10. The Alps (page 54).

Page 91 Guess the icon: 1. Clouded leopard (page 85), 2. Colossal squid (page 68), 3. 50,000 (page 42), 4. Green (page 12), 5. One year (page 56), 6. The Andes (page 24), 7. 75 cm or 29½ in (page 56), 8. Common wombat (page 79), 9. Western deserts (page 14), 10. African spurred tortoise (page 37), 11. Congo Basin (page 31), 12. Giant ameiva (page 38), 13. Resplendent quetzal (page 16), 14. Narwhal (page 87), 15. Madagascar (page 43), 16. Great bustard (page 55), 17. Goliath birdeater (page 23), 18. Yellow-eyed penguin (page 11), 19. Monarch butterfly (page 17), 20. Vampire bat (page 71), 21. 10 cm or 4 in (page 71), 22. Wallace's flying frog (page 72), 23. Stag beetle (page 52).

Glossary

amphibians
Cold-blooded animals that live both on land and in water, such as frogs and newts

birds
Warm-blooded animals that are covered in feathers and have a bill, many of which can fly, such as eagles

climate
Normal weather pattern during the year in any part of the world

coniferous tree
Type of tree with cones and needle-like leaves that keeps its leaves all year round

continents
Seven large areas of land that the world is divided into: Africa, Antarctica, Asia, Australasia, Europe, North America, and South America

coral reefs
Rock-like structures formed by coral animals in the shallow waters along coasts

deciduous tree
Type of tree that loses its leaves in autumn or the dry season

desert
Dry region that gets very little rainfall in a year. Deserts can be hot or cold

endangered
Word used to describe a species of plant or animal with only a few living members left

Equator
Imaginary line around the middle of the Earth

extinct
Word used to describe a plant or animal species that has no living members

fish
Cold-blooded animals that live in water and have gills and fins, such as salmon

habitat
Environment in which an animal or plant lives

hibernation
Sleep-like state some animals enter in winter

invertebrates
Cold-blooded animals without a backbone, such as insects, spiders, or squids

island
Piece of land that has water all around it

mammals
Warm-blooded animals that have hair and feed their young with milk, such as mice

mangroves
Trees that live in salty water and have long, stilt-like roots

marsupial
Type of mammal that keeps its young in a pouch

migration
Movement of a large number of animals from one area to another. Animals migrate to follow warmer weather and to find food

mountain
Area of land that rises up much higher than the land around it to form a peak

national park
Area of countryside that has been preserved in its natural state by the government of a country to protect the wildlife there and for people to enjoy

native
Word used to describe an animal that comes from a particular area or country

nocturnal
Word used to describe animals that are awake during the night

ocean
Very large sea. There are five oceans: the Pacific, Atlantic, Indian, Arctic, and Southern

plain
Area of flat land with few trees, often covered with grass

plateau
Large area of high, flat land

polar regions
Areas within the polar circles. Polar regions are covered in snow and ice for most of the year and are extremely cold

predator
Animal that hunts other living animals for food

prey
Animal that is hunted for food

rainforests
Dense forests with very high rainfall. Most are near the Equator and are also very hot

reptiles
Cold-blooded animals with dry, scaly skin, such as snakes, tortoises, and crocodiles

scrubland
Area of land covered in different types of grass, and small trees and bushes

species
Particular group of animals or plants that share similar features

taiga
Area of cold, coniferous forest found near the Arctic Circle

temperate grassland
Large areas of grass found in regions with hot and cold seasons, such as prairie, steppe, and pampas

temperate regions
Areas with hot and cold seasons found between tropical and polar regions

tropical grassland
Large areas of grass found in areas that are hot all year round, such as savanna and cerrado

tropical regions
Areas that are hot all year round, found near the Equator between the Tropic of Cancer and the Tropic of Capricorn

tundra
Cold, treeless plains found near the Arctic Circle

wetlands
Land with wet, spongy soil, such as a marsh or swamp

Index

A

aardvarks 42, 44
acacia trees 34, 41
Afghanistan 60, 64, 65
Africa 34–45
Alaska 10
Albania 47, 52, 57
albatrosses 84
Algeria 34, 36
alligators 18
The Alps 54
Amazon rainforest 20, 22–23
Amazon River 21
Andes 21, 24–25, 32–33
Andorra 46
Angola 34–35, 40, 42
anhingas 18
Antarctic Circle 6
Antarctica 84–85
anteaters 22, 30
antelopes 12, 36, 37, 41, 42, 45, 62, 65, 67, 69, 70, 75
ants 23, 30, 52
Arabian Peninsula 60, 70
Arctic 86–87
Arctic Circle 6
Argentina 20, 25, 26–27
armadillos 15, 31
Armenia 60, 65
Asia 60–75
Asian steppe 64
assassin bugs 26
asses 67, 74
Atlantic Ocean 88
Australasia 76–83
Australia 76, 78–79, 82–83
Austria 46, 52, 54
aye-ayes 43
Azerbaijan 60, 65

B

baboons 40, 70
badgers 10, 50, 59
Bahamas 9, 17
Bahrain 60, 70
Bangladesh 61, 67
baobabs 43
barracudas 18
barrier islands 9
batfish 17
bats 17, 48, 53, 59, 72, 80
bears 8, 10, 13, 24, 33, 47, 62, 66, 71, 73, 86
beavers 11, 59
bee-eaters 39
bees 51
beetles 22, 41, 52
Belarus 47, 48, 53, 55, 58–59
Belgium 46, 52
Belize 9, 16

Benin 34
bharals 67
Bhutan 61, 67
Białowieża Forest 58–59
birch trees 62
birds of paradise 73
bison 8, 12, 59
blue tits 52
bobcats 14
Bolivia 20, 23, 24, 28, 30
bongos 38
bonobos 38
boobies 29
Borneo 61, 72
Bosnia & Herzegovina 47, 52, 57
Botswana 40, 42
Brazil 20–21, 22–23, 24, 28, 30–31
British Isles 46, 50–51, 52
brittle stars 85
Brunei 61, 73
buffaloes 38, 72
Bulgaria 47, 55, 57
Burkina Faso 34
Burundi 35
bushbabies 40
bustards 37, 55, 75
butterflies 11, 22, 54, 68

C

cacti 15
caimans 28
The Camargue 46
Cambodia 61, 72
camels 35, 37, 60, 75
Cameroon 34, 38
Canada 8–9, 10–11, 12–13, 86
Cape Verde 34
capercaillies 49
capybaras 20, 28
caracals 70
caracaras 25, 33
cardinals 13
Caribbean 9, 17
Carpathian Mountains 47
Caspian Sea 64
cats 15, 27, 31, 64, 70
centipedes 56
Central African Republic 34–35, 38
Central America 9, 16
Central Asian deserts 65
Cerrado 30–31
Chad 34–35, 37, 38
chameleons 43, 56
chamois 54
chapis 38
cheetahs 42, 45
cherry trees 69
chickens 12
Chihuahuan Desert 15
Chile 20, 25
chimpanzees 39

China 60, 61, 64, 65, 66–67, 68–69, 72, 74–75
chinchillas 25
chipmunks 63
choughs 54
clams 83
climatic zones 6
clownfish 83
coatis 23
cock-of-the-rocks 25
cod 83, 86
colocolos 32
Colombia 20, 22, 24
Comoros 35
condors 25, 32
Congo 34, 38
Congo Basin 38–39
continents 6–7
coral 82
coral reefs 77, 82–83
Cordillera Blanca 32–33
cork oaks 57
cormorants 29
Corsica 56
Costa Rica 9, 16
coyotes 12
coypus 26
crabs 29, 51, 89
cranes 69
crayfish 81
Crete 57
Croatia 46, 52, 54, 57
crocodiles 17, 37, 79
crossbills 49
crows 49
Cuba 9, 17
cuckoos 56
culpeos 33
cuttlefish 88
Cyprus 60
Czech Republic 46, 52

D

damselflies 81
deer 8, 13, 24, 25, 27, 28, 32, 51, 53, 58, 62, 68
Democratic Republic of the Congo 35, 38, 40–41
Denmark 46, 52
desert broom 14
deserts 14–15, 35, 36–37, 42, 60, 65, 70, 74–75, 76, 78, 84
dingoes 79
dinosaur fossils 74
Djibouti 35
dogs 25, 31, 40, 58, 69, 79
dolphins 22, 73, 81, 89
Dominican Republic 9, 17
dormice 51, 53
ducks 33, 49, 68, 69
dugongs 82

E

eagles 8, 12, 23, 39, 45, 49, 55, 64
East Asian forests 68–69
East Timor 61, 73
Eastern forests 13
echidnas 79
Ecuador 20, 22, 24
eels 23
Egypt 35, 37
El Salvador 9, 16
elephants 40, 45, 71
emus 78
England 51
Equator 6
Equatorial Guinea 34
Eritrea 35, 37
Estonia 47, 48, 52
Ethiopia 35, 37
Europe 46–59
European forests 52–53
European steppe 55
The Everglades 18–19

F

falcons 64
Falkland Islands 21, 25
Fiji 77
Finland 47, 48, 52, 87
fireflies 11
flamingos 21, 24, 41
Florida 18–19
footballfish 88
forests 13, 22–23, 35, 52–53, 58–59, 68–69, 71, 77
  see also rainforests; taiga
fossas 43
foxes 12, 13, 26, 36, 52, 58, 65, 67, 87
France 46, 52, 54, 56
French Guiana 21, 23
frigatebirds 17
frogs 16, 19, 22, 24, 26, 31, 39, 42, 43, 56, 63, 72, 80
fynbos 34

G

Gabon 34, 38
galagos 40
Galápagos 29
gallinules 19
The Gambia 34
gazelles 37, 65, 70, 75
geckos 36, 57
geese 11, 25, 32
geladas 35
Georgia 60
gerbils 65
Germany 46, 52, 54
Ghana 34
gibbons 72
giraffes 34, 41, 44

goats 65, 66, 69
Gobi Desert 74–75
gorals 69
gorillas 38
grasslands 30–31
  see also pampas; savanna; steppes
Great Barrier Reef 82–83
Great Plains 8, 12
Greece 47, 52, 57
Greenland 9, 87
grisons 27
guanacos 32
Guatemala 9, 16
Guinea 34
guinea pigs 24
Guinea-Bissau 34
Guyana 21, 23

H

habitats 5, 6
Haiti 9, 17
hamsters 55
hares 12, 48, 65, 66, 87
hawks 29
heather 46
hedgehogs 50, 65
herons 18
Himalayas 61, 66–67
hippopotamuses 40, 44
hogs 39
Honduras 9, 16
honey badgers 44
hoopoes 53
hornbills 41
hornets 71
horses 46, 60, 64, 70, 75
hummingbirds 15, 16, 33
Hungary 47, 52
hutias 17
hyenas 36
hyraxes 70

I

ibexes 54, 56
icefish 84
Iceland 46, 48
iguanas 29, 30
impalas 41, 45
India 60, 66, 71, 72
Indian forests 71
Indian Ocean 89
Indonesia 61, 73
Iran 65, 70
Iraq 60, 70
Ireland 46, 51
Israel 60, 70
Italy 46, 52, 54, 57
Ivory Coast 34

J

jackals 57
jaguars 23
Jamaica 9, 17
Japan 61, 69
jays 49
jellyfish 83
jerboas 37, 74
Jordan 60, 70

K

kakapos 81
Kalahari Desert 42
kangaroos 77, 78
kapok trees 22
kauri trees 80
Kazakhstan 60, 64, 65
keas 81
Kenya 35
kererus 81
kiangs 67
kingfishers 27, 78
Kiribati 77
kites 19, 51
kiwis 80
koalas 79
komodo dragons 73
kookaburras 78
Kosovo 47, 52, 57
krill 85
Kruger National Park 44–45
Kuwait 60
Kyrgyzstan 60, 64, 65

L

ladybirds 51
Laos 61, 72
Latvia 47, 48, 52
Lebanon 60
lemmings 48, 86, 87
lemurs 43
leopards 38, 61, 67, 68
Lesotho 35
Liberia 34
Libya 34–35, 37
lichen 86
Liechtenstein 46
lions 40, 45
Lithuania 47, 48, 52
lizards 14, 26, 29, 30, 31, 36, 56, 70, 72, 73, 78
llamas 24
locust 36
loons 11
lungfish 39
Luxembourg 46, 52
lynxes 48, 57

M

macaws 9, 30
Macedonia 47, 52, 55, 57
Madagascar 35, 43
magpies 57
Majorca 56
Malawi 35
Malaysia 61, 72
Mali 34, 36
Malta 57
manakins 30
mandrills 38
mantises 72
maras 26
marlins 17
marmots 54, 64, 66, 74
Marshall Islands 77
Mauritania 34, 36
Mauritius 35
meadowlarks 27
Mediterranean scrubland 56–57
Mediterranean Sea 47, 56–57
meerkats 42
Mexico 8–9, 15
mice 51, 53, 55, 59, 66
Micronesia 76
midges 85
millipedes 52
minks 52
Mojave Desert 14, 15
Moldova 47, 53
mole rats 55
moles 55
Monaco 46
Mongolia 60, 61, 68, 74–75
mongooses 71
monkeys 16, 23, 28, 41, 56, 68, 69, 70, 73
Montenegro 47, 52, 57
moorland 46
moose 11, 47
Morocco 34, 36
mosquitoes 39
moss 46
moths 43, 57
mountains 8, 24–25, 35, 54, 61, 66–67
Mozambique 35, 41
musk oxen 86
mussels 88
Myanmar (Burma) 61, 67, 72

N

Namibia 34–35, 40, 42
Nauru 77
Nepal 60, 66
Netherlands 46, 52
New Zealand 77, 80–81
newts 55
Nicaragua 9, 16

Niger 34, 37
Nigeria 34, 37
nightingales 55
nightjars 52
North America 8–19
North Korea 61, 69
North Pole 87
Northern Ireland 51
Norway 46, 48, 52, 87

O

oaks 51, 57
oceans 88–89
ocelots 16
octopuses 89
okapis 38
Oman 60, 70
onagers 64
opossums 13, 31
orangutans 61, 72
ospreys 49
ostriches 42
otters 10, 28, 51
Outback 76
owls 11, 13, 15, 27, 48, 51, 53, 59, 63, 81, 87

P

Pacific Ocean 88–89
Pakistan 60, 65, 66, 71
Palau 76
pampas 21, 26–27
pampas grass 27
Panama 9, 16
pandas 67
pangolins 39
Pantanal 20, 28
panthers 19
Papua New Guinea 76, 79
Paraguay 21, 23, 28, 30
parrots 38, 81
partridges 70
Patagonia 21
peafowl 71
pelicans 57, 76
penguins 29, 76, 81, 84, 85
Peru 20, 22, 24, 32–33
petrels 85
pheasants 69
Philippines 61, 73
pigeons 53, 81
pigs 17, 39, 56
pine martens 54, 58
piranhas 23
plankton 89
platypuses 79
Poland 47, 52, 58–59
polar bears 86

polar zones 6, 7
polecats 55, 64, 74
ponies 9
porcupine fish 89
porcupines 42
porpoises 51
Portugal 46, 56
possums 78, 79
prairie dogs 8, 12
prairie shoestring 12
ptarmigans 54
Puerto Rico 9, 17
puffins 48
pumas 15

Q

Qatar 60, 70
quetzals 16

R

rabbits 12, 14, 56
raccoons 13, 69
rafflesia flowers 72
rainforest 9, 20, 38–39, 61, 72–73
rats 15
rays 73, 88
Red Sea 35, 37
redwood trees 8
reindeer 86
rheas 21, 26
rhinoceroses 40, 71, 72
roadrunners 15
robins 51, 63
Romania 47, 52, 55, 57
rubythroats 63
Russian Federation 47, 48–49, 53, 55,
 60–61, 68–69, 86
Rwanda 35

S

sables 62
Sahara Desert 35, 36–37
salamanders 54, 68
salmon 10, 88
salmonberries 10
Samoa 77
San Marino 46
sandgrouse 37
sardines 88
Sardinia 56
Saudi Arabia 60, 70
savanna 34, 40–41, 44, 60
saxaul trees 75
scorpions 37, 38
Scotland 46, 50
scrubland 56–57
sea anemones 83
sea breams 77

sea lions 29, 81
sea urchins 89
seagulls 60
seahorses 88
seals 47, 50, 63, 84, 87
seas 88–89
secretary birds 44
Senegal 34
Serbia 47, 52, 57
seriemas 31
serows 69
serratulas 66
Seychelles 35
sharks 78, 83, 87, 88, 89
sheep 14, 36, 63, 67
shrews 54
shrimps 83
Sicily 57
Sierra Leone 34
skuas 85
skunks 13
sloths 16, 71
Slovakia 47, 52
Slovenia 46, 52, 54
slugs 8, 82
snails 28, 80
snakes 12, 15, 18, 23, 24, 28, 30, 36, 51,
 53, 65, 68, 71, 73, 79, 83
Snares Islands 76
solenodons 17
Solomon Islands 77
Somalia 35
Sonoran Desert 15
South Africa 34–35, 42, 44–45
South America 20–33
South Korea 61, 69
South Pole 84
South Sudan 35, 38
Southeast Asian rainforest 72–73
Southern savanna 40–41
Spain 46, 56
spiders 14, 19, 23, 79
spiny forest 35
sponges 82
spoonbills 28
spruce trees 49
squid 85
squirrels 13, 50, 59, 62, 64, 71
Sri Lanka 60, 71
starfish 82
starlings 55
steppes 21, 55, 64
stick insects 24
stingrays 73
stoats 49
storks 28
sturgeon 89
Sudan 35, 37

sugar gliders 79
sugar maples 13
sunbirds 72
sunfish 18
Suriname 21
Swaziland 35
Sweden 46, 48, 52, 87
Switzerland 46, 52, 54
Syria 60

T

tahrs 66
taiga 10–11, 47, 48–49, 62–63
Taiwan 61, 73
Tajikistan 60, 64, 65
tamarins 22
tangs 82
Tanzania 35
tapirs 16
tarsiers 73
tayras 16
temperate zones 6, 7
tenrecs 43
termites 31
terns 86
Thailand 61, 72
thorny devils 78
Tibetan Plateau 66–67
tigers 62, 71
toads 49, 58, 67
Togo 34
Tonga 77
toothfish 84
tortoises 14, 29, 37, 43, 57, 64
toucans 23
Trinidad and Tobago 9, 17
trogons 17
Tropic of Cancer 6
Tropic of Capricorn 6
tropical zone 6, 7
tuataras 81
tuna 88
tundra 86
Tunisia 34, 36
turacos 38
Turkey 47, 60
Turkmenistan 60, 65
turtles 10, 17, 18, 83, 89
Tuvalu 77

U

Uganda 35
Ukraine 47, 53, 55
United Arab Emirates 60, 70
United Kingdom 46, 50–51
United States of America (USA) 8–9, 10,
 12–15, 18–19, 86
Ural Mountains 49, 55

Uruguay 21, 27
Uzbekistan 60, 64, 65

V

Vanuatu 77
Vatican City 46
Venezuela 17, 20, 22
vicuñas 25
Vietnam 61, 72
viscachas 27, 32
voles 52
vultures 14, 30, 42, 44, 67

W

Wales 51
walruses 87
warthogs 42
water lilies 28
weasels 53, 67
weavers 42
Western deserts 14–15
Western Sahara 34, 36
wetas 80
wetlands 18–19, 20, 28, 46
whales 80, 84, 87, 88, 89
wild boars 47, 53
wildcats 50
wildebeests 41
witchetty grubs 78
wolverines 49
wolves 8, 10, 11, 30, 47, 56, 58, 66
wombats 79
woodpeckers 59, 63
world map 6–7

Y

yaks 61, 66
Yemen 60, 70

Z

Zambia 35, 40–41
zebras 40, 45
Zimbabwe 35, 41

Credits

Dorling Kindersley would like to thank Dr. Don E. Wilson, Curator Emeritus, Department of Vertebrate Zoology, National Museum of Natural History, Smithsonian, for his expert consultation.

The publisher would also like to thank the following people for their help in preparing this book: Kealy Gordon and Ellen Nanney at the Smithsonian; Helen Peters for the index; Polly Goodman for proofreading; Joylon Goddard and Katy Lennon for additional editing; and Jagtar Singh and Sachin Singh for additional design.

Picture Credits:

The publisher would also like to thank the following for their kind permission to reproduce their photographs:

(Key: a-above; b-below/bottom; c-centre; f-far; l-left; r-right; t-top)

8 Alamy Stock Photo: John Hyde / Design Pics Inc (c). **iStockphoto.com:** ericfoltz (bl); Pawel Gaul (d). **9 iStockphoto.com:** John_Wijsman (tr); OGphoto (cr). **11 Alamy Stock Photo:** Danny Green / Nature Picture Library (tl); Vl_K (tr). **Dorling Kindersley:** Jerry Young (br). **12 123RF.com:** wrangel (br). **Corbis:** Ocean (d). **13 123RF.com:** Marie-Ann Daloia (cr). **Dorling Kindersley:** Jerry Young (tl). **14 Alamy Stock Photo:** Wayne Lynch / All Canada Photos (tc). **SuperStock:** Cyril Ruoso / Minden Pictures (d). **16 Fotolia:** Eric Isselee (d). **17 Photolibrary:** Photodisc / Tom Brakefield (tr). **18 Alamy Stock Photo:** WaterFrame_eda (d). **Dorling Kindersley:** Jerry Young (cr). **Dreamstime.com:** Brian Lasenby (cb). **Getty Images:** Joe McDonald / Corbis Documentary (bl). **18-19 Getty Images:** Tim Graham / Getty Images News. **19 Alamy Stock Photo:** George Grall / National Geographic Creative (bl). **iStockphoto.com:** FernandoAH (tl); madcorona (crb); hakoar (tr); ygluzberg (d). **20 Alamy Stock Photo:** Denis-Huot Michel / hemis.fr / Hemis (bl). **iStockphoto.com:** Marcelo Horn (d). **21 123RF.com:** belikova (b). **Alamy Stock Photo:** blickwinkel / Wothe (cr). **iStockphoto.com:** Magaiza (tr). **22 iStockphoto.com:** Leonardo Prest Mercon Ro / LeoMercon (d). **23 123RF.com:** Anan Kaewkhammul (br). **Alamy Stock Photo:** Amazon-Images (cra). **24 SuperStock:** Albert Lleal / Minden Pictures (tc). **25 Dorling Kindersley:** Blackpool Zoo (br). **iStockphoto.com:** webguzs (bl). **26 SuperStock:** Juniors (d). **27 Alamy Stock Photo:** Johner Images (tr). **Dorling Kindersley:** Gary Ombler (br). **28 123RF.com:** Francisco de Casa Gonzalez (br); Ondřej Prosický (tr). **Alamy Stock Photo:** James Brunker (bl). **29 123RF.com:** mark52 (bl). **Alamy Stock Photo:** Reinhard Dirscherl (cr). **30 Dorling Kindersley:** Greg Dean / Yvonne Dean (d). **31 naturepl.com:** Luiz Claudio Marigo (br). **SuperStock:** Minden Pictures (cra). **32 123RF.com:** Martin Otero (d). **Dorling Kindersley:** Hanne Eriksen / Jens Eriksen (fcrb); Prof. Marcio Motta (cb). **Dreamstime.com:** Jeremy Richards (bl). **33 123RF.com:** Martin Schneiter (c). **Dorling Kindersley:** E. J. Peiker (tr). **Dreamstime.com:** Musat Christian (cr). **SuperStock:** Glenn Bartley / All Canada Photos (bl, tl). **34 Alamy Stock Photo:** Michele Burgess (bc); Lars Johansson (d).

35 Alamy Stock Photo: Ange (br); Aivar Mikko (tc). **iStockphoto.com:** helovi (cra). **36 Dorling Kindersley:** Jerry Young (br). **38 Dorling Kindersley:** Liberty's Owl, Raptor and Reptile Centre, Hampshire, UK (bl). **39 123RF.com:** Andrey Gudkov (cr); Jatesada Natayo (tr). **41 123RF.com:** pytyczech (bc). **Alamy Stock Photo:** Andrew Mackay (r). **42 Dorling Kindersley:** Wildlife Heritage Foundation, Kent, UK (bl). **Dreamstime.com:** Artushfoto (ftr). **SuperStock:** Alexander Koenders / NiS / Minden Pictures (tr). **43 Alamy Stock Photo:** Travel Africa (d); Eric Nathan (br). **Dreamstime.com:** Faunuslsd (bl). **44 Depositphotos Inc:** Meoita (cb). **Dorling Kindersley:** Blackpool Zoo, Lancashire, UK (crb). **Dreamstime.com:** Lauren Pretorius (bl). **SuperStock:** Biosphoto (d); Roger de la Harpe / Africa (c). **45 Dorling Kindersley:** Suzanne Porter / Rough Guides (fcra). **Dreamstime.com:** Clickit (c); Ecophoto (tr); Rixie (cra); Mark De Scande (cr); Fabio Lamanna (bc). **46 Dreamstime.com:** Philip Bird (c). **iStockphoto.com:** nimu1956 (db). **47 Alamy Stock Photo:** Images & Stories (cr). **iStockphoto.com:** misterbike (tr); vencavolrab (bc). **49 Dorling Kindersley:** ZSL Whipsnade Zoo (tr). **Dreamstime.com:** Anagram1 (tl). **SuperStock:** Juniors (br). **50 123RF.com:** Piotr Krześlak (tc). **51 Dorling Kindersley:** Hoa Luc (br). **52 Dorling Kindersley:** British Wildlife Centre, Surrey, UK (bl). **53 123RF.com:** alucard21 (tr). **Dorling Kindersley:** Rollin Verlinde (bl). **54 Dorling Kindersley:** British Wildlife Centre, Surrey, UK (bl). **iStockphoto.com:** mauribo (br). **55 Dreamstime.com:** Mikelane45 (crb). **SuperStock:** Kurt Kracher / imagebro / imageBROKER (tr). **57 Dreamstime.com:** García Juan (tr); Rosemarie Kappler (tl). **58 Dorling Kindersley:** British Wildlife Centre, Surrey, UK (cr, c); Jerry Young (d). **Dreamstime.com:** Valentino2 (bl). **58-59 Alamy Stock Photo:** Aleksander Bolbot. **59 123RF.com:** alein (tc); Alexey Sokolov (bl). **Dorling Kindersley:** Rollin Verlinde (ftr). **Fotolia:** Eric Isselee (cr). **60 Alamy Stock Photo:** Danita Delimont / Gavriel Jecan (d); Ethiopia / Panther Media GmbH (bl). **iStockphoto.com:** Danielrao (tr). **61 Alamy Stock Photo:** Art Wolfe / Cultura RM (cr). **iStockphoto.com:** fotoVoyager (tr). **62 123RF.com:** Sergey Krasnoshchokov (d). **Dorling Kindersley:** Blackpool Zoo (bl). **63 Dreamstime.com:** Silviu Matei (tl). **iStockphoto.com:** Gerdzhikov (br). **64 Dorling Kindersley:** Twan Leenders (tr). **65 Dreamstime.com:** Dmytro Pylypenko (tl). **66 Dreamstime.com:** Rudra Narayan Mitra (bc). **67 Dorling Kindersley:** Connor Daly (tr); Wildlife Heritage Foundation, Kent, UK (b). **68 Dreamstime.com:** Vasiliy Vishnevskiy (bl). **iStockphoto.com:** Biscut (d). **69 Dorling Kindersley:** Jerry Young (br). **70 123RF.com:** Shlomo Polonsky (bl); wrangel (br). **Alamy Stock Photo:** blickwinkel / McPHOTO / MAS (tr). **71 123RF.com:** tonarinokeroro (cra). **SuperStock:** Biosphoto (br). **72 Dreamstime.com:** Phittavas (tl). **73 123RF.com:** aquafun (tr). **74-75 Alamy Stock Photo:** David Tipling Photo Library. **74 Dreamstime.com:** Evgovorov (bl). **naturepl.com:** Roland Seitre (cb). **SuperStock:** Biosphoto (cra, cr); Pete Oxford / Minden Pictures (crb); Stock Connection (d). **75 Dreamstime.com:** Mikelane45 (tc);

Maxim Petrichuk (bl). **iStockphoto.com:** muha04 (cra). **SuperStock:** Biosphoto (ca). **76 Alamy Stock Photo:** David Foster (db); Schöttger / mauritius images GmbH (cla); Frans Lanting Studio (bc). **77 Alamy Stock Photo:** WaterFrame_fba (tr). **SuperStock:** Roland Seitre / Minden Pictures (tl). **78 Alamy Stock Photo:** FLPA (br). **79 Fotolia:** Eric Isselee (br). **80 Getty Images:** Robin Bush / Oxford Scientific (bl). **81 123RF.com:** petervick167 (tl). **82 123RF.com:** Daniel Poloha (br). **Alamy Stock Photo:** Barry Brown / DanitaDelimont.com / Danita Delimont (c). **Dreamstime.com:** Izanbar (d). **iStockphoto.com:** LeventKonuk (bl). **SuperStock:** Fred Bavendam / Minden Pictures (tr); Ron Offermans / Buiten-beeld / Minden Pictures (cr). **82-83 Alamy Stock Photo:** Norbert Probst / imageBROKER. **83 123RF.com:** antos777 (da). **Alamy Stock Photo:** Reinhard Dirscherl (br). **Dreamstime.com:** Carol Buchanan (bc); Apidech Ninkhlai (tc); Whitcomberd (tr). **SuperStock:** Fred Bavendam / Minden Pictures (db, ftl, tl); D. Parer & E. Parer-Cook / Minden Pictures (fbl). **84 Alamy Stock Photo:** David Osborn (bl). **85 Getty Images:** Bill Curtsinger / National Geographic (tr); David Tipling / Digital Vision (br). **86 123RF.com:** Ondřej Prosický (da). **87 Alamy Stock Photo:** Arco / G. Lacz / Arco Images GmbH (tr). **Dorling Kindersley:** Jerry Young (br). **88 iStockphoto.com:** BulentBARIS (tc). **89 Dreamstime.com:** Igor Dolgov (tr).

All other images © Dorling Kindersley

For further information see: **www.dkimages.com**